FROM SUBJECTIVE EXPERIENCE
TO CULTURAL CHANGE

This book emphasizes the evolving rather than homeostatic aspects of human behavior. Beginning with theories of complexity and self-generation of behavior, Inghilleri emphasizes the central role of psychic functioning in the domain of biological and cultural evolution. Psychic processes, considered determined, autonomous, and generative with respect to the processes of biological and cultural evolution, are viewed in relation to greater processes of complexity and autonomy of organization. The theory of Self-Determination, developed by Deci and Ryan, and the theory of Flow, developed by Csikszentmihalyi, are considered from this point of view. In addition, the theoretical framework offered by Inghilleri is tested in specific fields: academia, creativity, mental health, and culture change processes.

Paolo Inghilleri is Professor of Social Psychology and Human Development at the University of Verona. He received both his M.D. and his Ph.D. in psychology from the University of Milan. His main areas of research include the relationship between biological, cultural and psychological processes, transcultural psychology, mental health and culture, and the experience of daily life.

FROM SUBJECTIVE EXPERIENCE TO CULTURAL CHANGE

ESPERIENZA SOGGETTIVA, PERSONALITÀ, EVOLUZIONE CULTURALE

Paolo Inghilleri

Translated by Eleonora Bartoli

CAMBRIDGE
UNIVERSITY PRESS

PUBLISHED BY THE PRESS SYNDICATE OF THE UNIVERSITY OF CAMBRIDGE
The Pitt Building , Trumpington Street, Cambridge, United Kingdom

CAMBRIDGE UNIVERSITY PRESS
The Edinburgh Building, Cambridge CB2 2RU, UK   http://www.cup.cam.ac.uk
40 West 20th Street, New York, NY 10011-4211, USA   http://www.cup.org
10 Stamford Road, Oakleigh, Melbourne 3166, Australia

© 1999 UTET- Libreria
via P. Giuria, 20 - 10125 TORINO

BF
701
.I5413
1999

First published in English 1999

Printed in the United States of America

Typeface Palatino 10/13.5   *System* QuarkXpress™ [HT]

A catalog record for this book is available from the British Library

Library of Congress Cataloging-in-Publication Data

Inghilleri, P. (Paolo)
   [Esperienza soggettiva a personalità. English]
   From subjective experience to cultural change / Paolo Inghilleri :
translated by Eleanora Bartoli.
     p. cm.
   ISBN 0 521 64248 5
   1. Genetic psychology   2. Behavior evolution.   3. Social evolution.
4. Autonomy (Psychology).   5. Personality development. I. Title.
BF701.I6412 1999
180.18'5—dc21   96-45466
                                             CIP

ISBN 0 521 64248 5 hardback

CONTENTS

FOREWORD

Mihaly Csikszentmihalyi

Long ago the natural sciences achieved a universal language and a global network of information exchange, so that a new finding in astronomy, or chemistry, or biology is almost immediately noted, evaluated, and replicated in laboratories the world over. By contrast in the social sciences, U.S. scholars are nowadays generally unaware of what their colleagues in other nations are doing. Because anthropology, sociology and psychology rely heavily on language and cultural context for describing and explaining their findings, it is often difficult to understand the significance of foreign scholarship, even on those rare occasions when it appears in English translation.

There are, of course, exceptions: In the past half century or so, the works of Levy-Strauss, Piaget, Vigotsky, and a few others have had a pervasive influence on American social science. But our assimilation of foreign thought has been quite selective: Only those scholars tend to be translated whose work is already congenial to an American readership. This is unfortunate, because one could argue that in the domain of the *Geistenwissenschaften* a multivocal, multicultural perspective advances knowledge more effectively than the homogeneous, hegemonic approach of the natural sciences. Regional accents might be jarring in mathematics, but in psychology they often greatly enrich our understanding of human experience by providing unusual perspectives and new possibilities.

Paolo Inghilleri provides one such enriching voice. Inghilleri, like his colleagues who were trained by Professor Fusto Massimini at the University of Milan, had his secondary schooling in the Liceo Classico, with its demanding curriculum heavy on ancient Greek, Latin and philosophy. After high school he went to and finished medical school, capping his M.D. with a specialization in psychology. Having concluded formal training, he began the series of cross-cultural field experiences that Professor Massimini expects of those who work in his laboratory. After a study of modernization in Egyptian nilotic villages and a series of brief visits to the Navajo reservation in the Southwest of the United States, Inghilleri began work in more third-world cultures than many people could name. Under the auspices of the Italian government and various private foundations, he did research in India and Thailand, and helped restore the mental health infrastucture in Nicaragua, Somalia, and other countries that, after the withdrawal of Soviet-style Russian psychiatric advisors, wanted to go back to a more cultural context-friendly way of treating their native patients.

This painstakingly acquired and diverse background is well reflected in *From Subjective Experience to Cultural Change*. First of all, the classical training shines through the serenely proportioned conceptual architecture. In reading Inghilleri, as some others of his compatriots, one has the sense that the thoughts on the page are carefully distilled from a great mass of information. As in good Italian design, one gets only the essential, presented with an easy elegance that satisfies while refreshingly omitting unnecessary details.

The medical training is evident in the grasp of the biological foundations of behavior, and especially of that evolutionary framework that underlies the argument of the book. But Inghilleri is aware – and here the multicultural experience becomes crucial – that evolution does not end with instructions encoded on chromosomes. Symbols, ideas, values, and techniques passed on through learning influence our behavior as much as genes do. There are great differences between information stored in chemicals and that stored in cultural artifacts; the latter changes, is selected, and gets transmitted in ways that can be understood more clearly from the perspective of the variation, selection, and transmission of genes.

But how does this cultural evolution proceed? Drawing on the latest advances in contemporary psychology as well as on the work of the Milan laboratory, Inghilleri develops the insight first glimpsed by Fausto Massimini: it is *psychological selection* that replicates cultural information. By focusing attention differentially on the contents of consciousness, each generation selects and preserves ideas and practices that will constitute the cultural milieu for the following generation. Each individual is shaped by how attention was used in the past, and that person makes choices that will define the future.

The most important contribution of this book is to explicate one central aspect of this process of psychological selection, involving autonomy and intrinsic motivation. There are many reasons for endorsing a particular technology or religious practice: because it saves time, or it is easier than others, or because it gives us more physical or psychological power. But the most interesting reasons for doing something are the intrinsic rewards we experience in doing it. The joy of the artist or scientist opening up new perspectives on reality, the joy of the athlete pushing the body beyond its limits, of the explorer discovering new lands, or that of parents who see their children grow, are prototypes of the state of consciousness in which we focus attention because we want the experience to continue. When such intrinsic rewards can be obtained from the roles of everyday life, from work as well as from leisure, the replication of a culture acquires a special dimension. The growth of individual complexity then becomes synchronized with the evolution of the culture.

This is the message of Inghilleri's work. Parts of it might be familiar to U.S. readers, but even for those who know the details, the synthesis that he achieves will be enlightening, especially at this time when a theory of positive psychology is trying to emerge from the disease-based, pathologically inspired model of human functioning that has held center-stage for so long. I hope you enjoy reading and thinking about this book as much as I have.

PREFACE

THIS BOOK AIMS TO PROVIDE THE READER WITH A CRITICAL, synthetic, and systematic overview of theories concerning psychological complexity, self-generation of behavior, and personality development.

Developed in the United States (in Rochester and Chicago, respectively), Deci's and Ryan's self-determination theory and Csikszentmihalyi's optimal experience or flow theory are well-known in psychology. Indeed, they have brought many researchers to gather data and develop models and hypotheses regarding behavioral responses, motivational processes, and experiential states. However, these theories reveal their proper meaning only when considered from a wider perspective. Hence our overarching question is: How ought the above-mentioned theoretical contributions be inserted into a more general conceptual framework?

An initial development of these contributions is provided by considering general theories concerning the complexity and self-generation of behavior. Starting from evidence and data derived from other disciplines, such as biology and physics, we will emphasize psychological theories highlighting evolving, rather than homeostatic, aspects of behavior in order to avoid theoretical reductionism. Chapter 1 offers a series of reflections on this issue. It also elaborates on those conceptions that emphasize the central role of psychic functioning in the domain of biological and cultural evolution. By *culture* we mean the whole of human artifacts, from objects of daily use, to laws, to academic or political institutions.

This central role of psychic functioning needs to be viewed as two sets of mutually determining processes. On the one hand, biology and culture evolve due to numerous moments of daily psychological selection, meaning moments of specific organizations of experience by virtue of which individuals select, internalize, and transmit the biocultural information at hand. On the other hand, individuals inherit biological and cultural instructions, and challenges from previous generations, thus constructing their own personalities. Psychic functioning, a bridge between personality, biology, and culture, is therefore at the same time determined, autonomous, and generative with respect to the two processes of biological and cultural evolution. Chapter 2 (itself broadly theoretical) and Chapter 3 (which analyze specific moments and contexts of behavioral development) are both concerned with this issue.

By taking into consideration these two elements – i.e., the central role of psychic processes and of subjective experience in biological and cultural evolution, and the tendency of the psychic world toward complexity and autonomy of organization – the two theories considered in Chapter 2 will find their proper dimension. In this way, they may not only help to further understand certain aspects of personality formation, but may also help to explain the connection between individual and social environment as it takes place, for instance, in academic institutions, in creativity, in mental health, and in meaningful examples of individual change and social adaptation.

ACKNOWLEDGMENTS

THIS BOOK IS THE RESULT OF SEVERAL YEARS OF RESEARCH THAT would not have taken place without the presence and the dear and knowledgeable help of two extraordinary researchers and friends: Fausto Massimini of the University of Milan and Mihaly Csikszentmihalyi of The University of Chicago. To them goes all of my gratitude and affection.

I would also like to thank Paolo Calegari of the University of Verona and Antonella Delle Fave of the University of Milan for their important scientific suggestions and their friendly support. Moreover, Marcello Cesa-Bianchi of the University of Milan has been a constant point of reference. A special thanks goes to Eleonora Bartoli (graduate student at The University of Chicago), the translator of this book, for her intelligence and her passionate curiosity. I would also like to thank James Governale for additional help with the translation. A loving thank you, at last, goes to my extended family, and in particular to Tuli, my wonderful companion.

1

BASIC CONCEPTS

1.1 A GENERAL PROBLEM OF PSYCHOLOGICAL THEORIES: THE RISK OF REDUCTIONISM

TODAY, REFLECTION ON THE STATUS OF CONTEMPORARY PSY-chology is particularly lively. Journals such as *New Ideas in Psychology* have been created primarily to emphasize emerging theories and critical evaluations of the subject (Baer, 1987; Bakan, 1987; Krantz, 1987). Within this discourse, general systematic contributions seem to be of particular interest. For instance, Gardner (1992), reviewing synthetically the history of the behavioral sciences, recalls that in 1780 Immanuel Kant identified three obstacles, at the time considered insurmountable, that prevented psychology from becoming a science. First, the mind is intrinsically modified when it studies itself. Second, the mind does not have a spatial dimension within which it can be studied. Third, there is no mathematical basis on which a science of the mind might be built. Hence Kant concluded:

[Psychology] can, therefore, never become anything more than a historical (and as such, as much as possible) systematic natural doctrine of the internal sense, i.e., a natural description of the soul, but not a science of the soul, nor even a psychological experimental doctrine (cf. Watson, 1979, p.88).

Over the course of the following two centuries, an impressive series of intellectual efforts, creative investigations, and systematic research discredited to a great extent the expectations of the German philosopher. Theories and schools, such as functionalism, structuralism, behaviorism, Gestalt psychology, and psychoanalysis, have

1

gradually conquered the academic world and public recognition. Psychology, along this arduous and partially unfinished journey toward becoming a unified science, was always interconnected with other disciplines. We may recall, first of all, the influence of the physical sciences on the first studies of perception, on Freud's thought in general, and on psychoanalytic concepts such as libido or discharge of energy. More recently, psychology has had to face the challenge of its comparison with neuroscience, based on molecular biology, and with the cognitive sciences, tied to artificial intelligence. For some scholars (Gardner, 1992), this comparison can even bring about the disappearance of psychology as a discipline in its own right, in that it may run the risk of being absorbed by either of the two previously mentioned disciplines. Another relatively recent area of confluence is anthropology, with the consequent development of disciplines such as cultural psychology (Shweder, 1990) and cross-cultural psychology (Berry, Poortinga, Segall and Dasen, 1992), which (particularly the latter) try to reconcile the study of cultural variables with the exactness of scientific methodology.

The historical course of the behavioral sciences developed along two (partially connected) major lines: (1) the recognition of the validity of experimental methodology belonging to the exact sciences – and in connection with it, the primacy of the principle of linear causality between the phenomena studied; (2) the study of psychological events in controlled settings (such as scientific laboratories) and professional and clinical practices. These facts brought about various consequences, in particular:

1. The overestimation of modern Western thought, with the consequent underestimation of the study of categorical systems and modes of constructing knowledge belonging to other cultures (even of great intellectual weight, such as the Chinese, Indian, or Japanese cultures). This is a tendency confirmed by the fact that subjects in experimental research and patients in clinical settings were, in the great majority of cases, white citizens of Western countries.

2. The frequent renunciation of a more direct study of behavior in real-life contexts and, contrarily, the strong emphasis on

2

studying the regularities emerging from pathological behaviors that, being pathological, make their generalization to the normal population difficult.

Generally speaking, these factors (the tie with other disciplines, which, except for anthropology, are to be counted among the exact sciences in the traditional sense; and the effort to conform to scientific methodology) brought about a series of epistemological dangers, above all the danger of *reductionism.*

These theories commonly view human action as the result (virtually a vector) of forces external to the individual: given a certain condition, behavior x is expected. The conditions taken into consideration by the various approaches are different: they can be of a biochemical or pharmacological type (for instance, the number of a certain type of neurotransmitters); they can be derived from innate needs like hunger or thirst; they can consist of relational processes, such as the mechanism of libidinal repression, as in psychoanalysis; they can be connected to rewards or punishments supplied by the external environment, as in behaviorism. In all these cases, we are ultimately faced with a mechanistic approach: a behavior derives directly from preceding causal conditions, which will differ according to the theory in question, and both the causal conditions and the behavior represent the factors on which the subjective states of an individual organism, meaning the center of an experience, depend. In other words, most of the behavioral sciences do not consider the possibility of an autonomous and original action of the self. According to these mechanistic conceptions, the functioning of the self derives entirely from the action of external forces. Another common aspect of these reductionistic theories is the viewing of behavior as homeostatic: the circuit "need/drive/motivation/behavior/satisfaction or reduction of need," characteristic of several theories beginning with psychoanalysis, represents a model centered on the attainment of equilibrium as an ultimate aim.

Faced with such reductionist approaches, a broader line of thought was developed during the 1970s – one that does not betray the psychological tradition, and that simultaneously aims

3

at scientific rigor and at communicating with other disciplines, with the goal of widening its own paradigms. This book finds its place within this line of thought. The following considerations therefore stem from those areas of psychology that study behavior as an evolving phenomenon and that view as central the concept of the self as an independent causal agent. The action of the self is also seen in connection with external contexts, which is to say, in connection with the group to which it belongs and with the challenges offered by the social environment. Such an approach, which finds its remote origins in the work of William James (1890) and in George H. Mead (1934), is also grounded, as we were saying, in recent theoretical developments derived from the natural sciences, such as chemistry and biology. These theoretical developments, as we shall see, have the common peculiarity of emphasizing the meaning and importance both of the concept of complexity and the evolution of information.

We will now present briefly some of these theoretical approaches as they emerged from their respective disciplines. The reader will find here a common thread related to the emerging foundations for a theory of behavior as an evolving process.

1.2 NEW THEORIES: COMPLEXITY AND AUTONOMY

1.2.1 The Contribution of Jacques Monod

In 1970 Jacques Monod, a molecular biologist who received the Nobel Prize for medicine in 1965, pointed out in a systematic way the three general properties of living beings (Monod, 1971). Such characteristics make the latter, on the whole, different from any other entity in the universe.

1. **Teleonomy:** The first property is teleonomy. Due to this property, all living beings are

   objects endowed with a purpose or project, which at the same time they exhibit in their structure and carry out through their performances (Monod, 1971, p.9).

4

Consider the genetic information contained in the DNA of the first zygote of an embryo, the fruit of the union of a spermatozoon and an ovule.[1] The zygote represents the project that will manifest itself in the structure of the entire adult organism and that will realize itself through his or her functions. For instance, such functions might be an organ's metabolic processes, the creation of new individuals, or, in a wider sense, the realization of artificial products, such as a single object or an entire social structure (as in the case of the development of a familial institution, an accomplishment which can be defined as one of the main functions of the human species) (Dawkins, 1976).

2. **Autonomous morphogenesis:** The second property is autonomous morphogenesis. The living organism is a "self-constructing machine." (Monod, 1971, p.10) It does not depend on external forces, but it gives

> proof of an autonomous determinism: precise, rigorous, implying a virtually total "freedom" with respect to outside agents or conditions – which are capable, to be sure, of impeding this development, but not of governing or guiding it, not of prescribing its organizational scheme to the living object (*ibid.*, p.10–11).

3. **Reproductive invariance:** This third property consists of the capacity to reproduce and transmit the organism's information – the patrimony of genetic information – without variations. This patrimony represents a highly complex organization that is able to fully preserve itself over time. Through the reproductive system, and thanks to the characteristics of gametes (sexual cells), the genes are transmitted from generation to generation.

1.2.2 The Contribution of Richard Dawkins

The concepts proposed by Monod have been subsequently reconsidered and elaborated by the ethologist Richard Dawkins (1976, 1982). Dawkins points out the three characteristics that for millions of years enabled the genes to replicate genetic information.

1. **Fidelity:** The capacity to produce copies identical to the original. It should be noted that this concept is close to the concept of reproductive invariance.

2. **Fecundity:** The capacity to produce numerous copies. It should be noted that this concept does not presuppose the necessity of autonomous morphogenesis. An entity is said to be able to replicate information if it is able to do so repetitively and with precision, independent from being able to do it thanks to internal (as in the case of biological information endowed, as we have seen, with autonomous morphogenesis) or external forces. This concept will be important in what follows.

3. **Longevity:** The capacity to survive the time necessary to exhibit the preceding two qualities, which is to say, to be able to faithfully and repetitively replicate the original. In reality, longevity is also transgenerational in that these three properties allow the genes to transmits themselves, largely intact, for a number of years tending to infinity.

Dawkins points out other two important concepts:

1. **The distinction between vehicles and replicators:** The former contain the information transmitted over time; the latter consist in the information that is actually replicated from generation to generation. The former are represented, in the case of biology, by the organism's cells, the latter by the genetic information contained in the DNA. The former die (from biological generation to biological generation), the latter survive (from generation to generation).

2. **The distinction between genes and memes:** Dawkins shows how fidelity, fecundity, and longevity are the three general properties that make an excellent replicator, independent from the type of information actually handled.

6

In other words, the genes represent good replicators of a specific kind of information – namely, biological information. But there are other types of replicators concerned with other sorts of information. According to Dawkins, it is actually biological evolution that led to a second type of replicator. The extraordinary capacity of the human central nervous system, leading to the symbolic capacity for language, and the capacity to build long-standing artifacts led to the development of *memes*, a new type of replicator, or unit of transmission of information – in this case not biological, but cultural. The term was coined by Dawkins on the basis of the Greek root *mimeme* ("to replicate with the aim of imitation"), then shortened to meme in assonance with gene and in association with the concept of memory.

> Examples of memes are tunes, ideas, catch-phrases, clothes fashions, ways of making pots or of building arches. Just as genes propagate themselves in the gene pool by leaping from body to body via sperms and eggs, so memes propagate themselves in the meme pool by leaping from brain to brain via a process which, in the broad sense, can be called imitation (Dawkins, 1976, p.206).

It is necessary to mention two important corollaries: once formed, the patrimony of cultural information, thanks to a new replicator, is independent from, even though correlated with, the patrimony of biological information. In other words, there is not a regulatory hierarchical bond going from the biological to the cultural. We are now faced with two distinct systems of evolution of information: biological evolution and cultural evolution.

Furthermore, memes also can be either vehicles or replicators. For instance, a political idea represents a memic replicator, which can be transmitted over time. A book, in which that idea is presented and promoted, or even an individual's central nervous system, which shares and internalizes such an idea, are both examples of vehicles of memic information.

The replicators are therefore transmitted over time. But how does this process occur? And is it the same for memes and for

7

genes? In order to better understand this issue, it is useful to introduce two concepts that derive from the biological and physical sciences.

1.2.3 Positive Entropy and Negative Entropy, or Negentropy

The physical, inorganic world, the so-called *nonliving nature*, follows the second principle of thermodynamics, which is to say that it tends toward positive entropy. This principle claims that every macroscopic system, separated from an energetic source, evolves in a single direction: degeneration of its order. As mentioned by Monod (1971, pp.197–199), the principle was formulated for the first time, in purely thermodynamic terms, by Clausius in 1850 as a generalization of Carnot's theorem. The degeneration of energy, or increase in entropy, is a statistically predictable consequence of the random movements and collisions of molecules. If, for instance, two separate spaces having different temperatures are joined, the hot (which is to say fast) molecules and the cold (which is to say slow) molecules randomly shift from one space to the other, eliminating the difference in temperature between the two spaces. It should be noted that as a consequence of this entropic process, an increase in disorder and a loss of information occur. The slow and fast molecules, at first separated, are now mixed. The two spaces, which were initially distinguishable owing to their difference in temperature, are now identical. There is therefore a specific relationship between entropy and information (Monod, 1971): the more entropic the system, the less information is present.

In more concrete terms, the second principle of thermodynamics can also be illustrated by the following example. Let us imagine an artifact made of inorganic material, such as a computer – a sophisticated object, rich in information in its internal structure. Now imagine leaving it outside, exposed to the influence of the weather. After a certain amount of time the artifact will disintegrate, it will become rust, dust, and inert material. The artifact, abandoned without care, will go through an entropic process and will lose order and information. We shall speak about artifacts and their connection with human behavior again at a later time.

Several authors (Monod [1971], Miller [1970], and Prigogine [1976]), have also pointed out that living systems tend toward negative entropy, which is to say toward heterogeneity, and toward a steady increase in structural complexity and differentiation of functions. Miller clearly points out the characteristics of the two systems, the living and the nonliving one. The first is characterized by negentropy, information, signal, precision, form, regularity, configuration, order, organization, regular complexity, heterogeneity, improbability (i.e., only a single alternative correctly describes the form), and predictability. The second, however, is characterized by: entropy, uncertainty, disturbance, error, chaos, fortuitousness, lack of configuration, disorder, disorganization, irregular simplicity, homogeneity, probability (i.e., more than one alternative correctly describes the form), and unpredictability.

1.2.4 Self-Organization

Along this same theoretical line, Ilya Prigogine, a physicist, chemist, and Nobel Prize winner, developed a concept according to which all living systems are characterized by a single dynamic principle, the principle of self-organization.

A living organism is a system that organizes itself in that its order is not imposed by the external environment but is established by the system itself. In other words, systems that organize themselves have a certain degree of autonomy. They are strictly connected with their environment, and they continuously interact with it, but such an interaction does not determine their organization. They are self-organized (Prigogine, 1976).

This concept was then retaken by Maturana and Varela (1980), according to whom the notion of self-organization is based on the notions of organization and autonomy. They define *organization* as the set of relationships that define a system as a unit and that determine the dynamics of the interactions and transformations that such a unit can undergo. *Autonomy* is defined as the condition of subordination of all change to the maintenance of the organization. Living systems are capable of maintaining their identity by actively compensating for their deformations.

Hence, the concept of self-organization, pointed out also by Von Foerster (1985) and Morin (1985), entails the development of other concepts and properties already mentioned as belonging to the biological world, as, for instance, autonomous morphogenesis and negative entropy. As we have seen, the living universe with its evolution also brought about a sophisticated regulation of the nonliving universe; that is, the development of specific artificial products that we have called memes – vehicles and replicators. These have brought about a second hereditary process – cultural evolution.

1.2.5 The Status of Artifacts

At this stage it is necessary to further analyze the status of artifacts. The latter are, once again, entities that transport and replicate information. Their analysis will be carried out from the point of view of the concepts of entropy and negentropy.

The arrow of an Amazonian hunter, an agricultural utensil, a cooking pot, a desk, an industrial press, a building, an institution such as a political party or a religious organization, a legal code, a technology, or a music score: all of these elements are examples of artifacts, which is to say, of memes, produced by human beings and deposited in specific inorganic vehicles. They constitute the so-called *material culture* (Cloack, 1975) – a term that suggests their vehicles' aspect – or *extrasomatic culture*, which is to say, deposited outside the physical bodies of individual organisms (Massimini, 1993) – a term that also suggests the immaterial aspects of replicators: it includes both a book and the ideas contained in that book, or a flag and the ideas and values associated with the flag.

Considering all we have said, artifacts hold a dual status (Monod, 1971). They are located in an intermediate space between the nonliving and the living world. They are constituted by inorganic matter. Since they lack autonomous morphogenesis and self-organization, they submit to the second principle of thermodynamics and therefore tend towards disorder, homogenization, loss of information, and entropy. For example, if I do not clean and eventually repair a camera, or if I do not bring inside an agricultural utensil with the passing of time, such artifacts will be ruined, and as time goes on they will disintegrate.

But artifacts are the result of external forces exercised by the craftsman on the material from which they are constituted. Therefore, they reflect and contain the tendency toward complexity, organization, order, and information, which characterize the living world. They will thus tend to negentropy, whence the increase in complexity of artifacts: from the very first camera to the modern electronic machines; from obsidian weapons to the modern war machines; and so forth.

This double set of characteristics, proper to objects produced by living beings, can be exemplified by the image of a termite hill: this structure increases in height and internal complexity – until it reaches remarkable dimensions – for as long as it is inhabited and maintained by termites. Once abandoned it decays rapidly, heading in a clearly entropic direction.

This dual status holds also for complex artifacts, such as an institution, an ideology, or a legal code. If I do not take care of an organization and instead leave it to itself, if I do not maintain, day after day, a live interest in an idea, if I do not apply or conform continuously to laws, all these artifacts will tend to loose meaning, information, and order, and ultimately they will disappear.

It seems clear, therefore, that the destiny of the maintenance, reproduction, and distribution of the entities that we have called memes depends on the type of relationship between these and the living world (in particular human beings). This is true for all artifacts. The latter are entities unified by their being highly relevant for our daily existence (Douglas and Isherwood, 1979; Csikzentmihalyi and Rochberg-Halton, 1981): from the objects decorating a house to the laws of a nation, from the dress of a stylist to a television set. The behavioral sciences have always been focused on the relationship between the internal world, behavior and external objects, inanimate or social. One might think, for instance, of the first psychophysical studies, of the development of psychoanalysis, or of social psychological theories. Psychology, therefore, situates itself at the center of the fundamental relationship between the natural world and the artificial world. It also plays a basic role for the understanding of the mechanisms by means of which human biological and cultural systems develop and increase in complexity.

1.3 THE DIFFERENT KINDS OF TELEONOMY

We shall now continue to discuss the concept of teleonomy in order to better specify the complex relationships existing between biology, culture, and psychological processes.

1.3.1 Genetic Teleonomy

The definition of teleonomy and the general properties of living beings that we have previously mentioned allow us to outline the essential teleonomic project of biological systems. This project consists of transmitting from generation to generation the content of invariance proper to the species. Darwin's evolutionary paradigm and the most recent studies in modern theoretical biology show with some precision this tendency of genetic reproduction.

The application of this view to the behavioral sciences brought about the development, beginning in the mid-1970s, of the human sociobiological paradigm (among the numerous contributors we shall mention, Wilson, 1975; Lumsden and Wilson, 1981), which also developed in the domain of evolutionary psychology (Barkow, Cosmides and Tooby, 1992). According to these theories, human behavior – even in its more complex social forms – finds its roots and explanation in the advantages of the reproduction of the genes transported by given organisms. Cognitive schemata, types of relationships – such as altruistic, familial, or inter group – and emotional or motivational systems, are all understood and explained in terms of adaptive advantages, whether current or acquired by the organisms at the time of the formation of their biological basis. Such a theoretical formulation has been partially questioned, from the very beginning of the sociobiological debate, not only by numerous and important ethnographic and anthropological data (see, for instance, Sahlins, 1976), but also by the expansion of the concept of teleonomy to the domains of artifacts and culture.

1.3.2 Cultural Teleonomy

The repetitive reproduction over time of artificial forms and structures, and the constancy of order and information in the nonbiological world, indicate the presence of a second teleonomic system that concerns the human species. This is the cultural one, or, following Dawkins (1976), the reproduction and evolution of memes (for a literature review on this topic see: Massimini and Inghilleri, 1993). Each artifact contains a project represented in its very structures and realized through its performances.

The distinction between these two teleonomic projects – the biological and the cultural – suggest that a hierarchical relationship between the two is not predetermined. In other words, if the project proper to the living world is the transgenerational transmission of its information (genetic reproductive invariance), the project proper to the world of artifacts is the transgenerational transmission of a second and different type of information, the cultural one (memic reproductive invariance). Thus, there are two projects that, being distinct, do not presuppose the regulation of one by the other: the DNA does not regulate the reproduction of artifacts, as the artifacts do not regulate the reproduction of the DNA.

We have also seen that objects lack autonomous morphogenesis. Only application of external forces, which is to say, action exerted by human beings, allows for the realization of the teleonomic project, meaning the transmission over time of those artifacts. There might seem to be a sort of hierarchy according to which the living influences the nonliving world. However, looking into this matter at a deeper level will lead us to formulate a fundamental question that might cause us to doubt such a claim: In which way are genes, the biological information borne by a craftsman (a blacksmith molding metal, or an author writing a book), transmitted to an

13

artifact (to the molded metal or book)? Is it possible to point out the bridge across which biological information is transmitted to cultural information, thus regulating it? And at which level is this bridge situated? Is it to be found within the biological system itself?

Further examples widen and complicate the argument. There is also a deep hierarchical relationship between artifacts and the biological, with the former regulating the latter. One of the major causes of death in industrialized countries is car accidents, which is to say that the use of certain artifacts limits biological survival. Atomic arsenals are able to exterminate all forms of life on the planet. Human reproductive strategies are deeply regulated by culture: specific laws like the ones favoring small families in the contemporary People's Republic of China; or general styles and models of life, leading to a decrease in the number of births, a current problem in Western Europe and in Italy in particular.

In these cases, too, we have to ask ourselves, what is the actual mechanism by which given memes (for instance, Chinese law or the contemporary style of city life) genuinely influence the reproduction of genes? In fact, the system of biological information and the system of cultural information, taken individually, independently from their mutual relationships, are not able to transmit themselves over time in an autonomous way. We have also seen that the reproduction of artifacts, lacking autonomous morphogenesis, necessitates the exertion of external forces: in daily life, through specific acts and behaviors, individuals produce, maintain, and transmit ideas and artifacts to other individuals.

Several authors (see, Massimini and Inghilleri, 1993) have also pointed out that the same mechanism holds for biological reproduction. In other words, even genes do not reproduce themselves in an autonomous way: their organization and internal morphogenesis necessitate human acts and behaviors. A clear discussion of this concept can be found in Feldman and Cavalli-Sforza (1978), who point out that the history of population genetics has been contested in light of a fundamental error of perspective. This research has produced sophisticated mathematical theories regarding the evolution of genes. By means of dynamic models, it

14

has explained the genotypic frequencies observed in natural settings, as well as in laboratories. However, natural selection acts at a phenotypic level, that is, through the manifest behavior of individuals. Yet the evolutionary population genetics has formalized natural selection (and the consequent evolution of biological information) as if it acted at the genotypic level. But gametes do not come together by themselves, nor can the genetic material transported by them reproduce by itself. These events occur through behavioral sequences at the phenotypic level: as far as the human species is concerned, these involve the choice of a partner, courtship, mating, the foundation of a family, the care of children, and so on.

We can therefore formulate an initial answer to our questions. The mutual influence of biological and cultural information, and of the reproduction over time of both types of information, occurs by means of specific phenotypic behaviors. Whence emerges the centrality (for the understanding of biocultural phenomena) of the science studying human behavior: psychology.

1.3.3 Psychological Teleonomy

Psychologists have often pointed out, at least indirectly, the centrality of the mind for biocultural processes. Using the conceptual grid just proposed, the review of major theories (Mecacci, 1994) points out a unifying factor: namely, that the human central nervous system is a biocultural entity in which hereditary biological information and internalized and learned cultural information complement each other in order to reproduce genes and memes, or biological and cultural projects.

Our discussion also leads us to take into consideration the different theories from a teleonomic point of view. In other words, we can ask ourselves if psychic functioning is also characterized by a project represented in its structures (or in its organization) and realized through its performances.

We have seen that the teleonomic project in biology and culture consists in the transmission of their information over time. Such a transgenerational transmission of the content of invariance leads

15

to the regular and repetitive reproduction of certain forms and structures. Furthermore, fecundity, fidelity, and longevity of the replicators of information are accompanied by a tendency toward negative entropy for both culture and biology: that is, order, complexity, and differentiation of information. Can all of this also be found within psychic functioning?

The idea that the functioning of our central nervous system (CNS) is based on regularities and repetitiveness is at the very basis of the cognitive approach. The CNS is in fact considered an elaborator and organizer of information that, coming from both the inside and the outside, reaches a system already having its own organization. The cognitive sciences aim at defining the models that describe the regularities with which the CNS organizes incoming information. Some known and established concepts, such as the TOTE model (Miller, Galanter and Pribram, 1960), the script (Abelson, 1976), and the module (Fodor, 1983), represent other regularities that tend to reproduce themselves repetitively in our psychic functioning, and that constitute, according to this point of view, a basic organizational structure. The process of cognitive dissonance and its resolution can be understood as a further example of the invariance in psychic functioning. The constants, in this case, are represented by the following mutually related elements:

1. The existence of dissonant or incongruent relationships between cognitive elements at a decision-making moment;
2. The presence of such dissonance gives rise to pressures which tend to eliminate it and avoid increasing it;
3. The manifestation of these pressures in practice includes a change in behavior and cognition, and a cautious opening to new information and new opinions (Festinger, 1957).

The general characteristics of teleonomy (project/structure/functions) are also found in another branch of psychology, namely, psychoanalysis. The late Freud (1920) defines three psychic agents, the Id, the Ego, and the Super-Ego. They were not thought of as locations (like the prior definitions of conscious, preconscious, and

16

unconscious) but rather, as structures. They represent sets of contents and mental processes functionally connected to each other.

The fundamental project of the human psyche is the discharge of libidinal energy, or its transformation, in order for a low level of excitation to be maintained in the psychic system. The free energy circulating in the unconscious (primary process) is transformed into cathected energy circulating in the conscious and preconscious (secondary process). Freud (1922) calls this process "neutralization of instinctual energy," which is followed by the delaying of the discharge and a psychic elaboration of the excitation. The project is represented in the previously mentioned psychic structures and it is realized through their functions (as, for instance, the mechanisms of defense).

Even in the case of psychoanalysis, regularities and repetitions are therefore present at the level of structures and processes. The idea of regularity is corroborated by the concept of the developmental stages of the child, with which given sequences of internal and behavioral functioning are regularly associated.

In addition to psychoanalysis, in which we seem to perceive the presence of a teleonomic project concerning psychic functioning, other theories seem to suggest the idea of psychological teleonomy. These theories also point out the tendency of psychic functions and contents toward complexity and order.

Consider, for instance, Piaget's (1954) basic perspective: on the one hand, the author once more points out the regularities of cognitive processes and their invariant replication; on the other hand, he emphasizes the evolving progress and the increase of complexity and integration (and therefore order) of psychic functions. From the sensory-motor stage, through the pre-operational and concrete operational stages, up to the formal operational stage, the child achieves higher capacities for abstract reasoning. Each stage is based on and derives from the preceding one, utilizing the latter's functions and achievements. Each new experience is grafted onto what already exists. Such an evolving view of behavior (which considers the development of psychic functions and capacities as a process continuing throughout life) also characterizes large sections of contemporary psychology, from studies on

17

adolescence (Lutte, 1987; Palmonari, 1993) to gerontology (Cesa-Bianchi, 1987).

This tendency toward complexity, also found in other theoretical formulations, such as the Jungian concept of individuation (1928, 1939) and Maslow's concept of "self-actualization" (1968) leads us to consider more closely the possibility of a psychological teleonomy.

This brief review of some of the fundamental psychological theories necessarily opens the door for a deeper discussion to be elaborated in the following chapters. Here, we wish to introduce the concept of psychological teleonomy. As previously mentioned, psychic processes lie at the center of biological and cultural teleonomy, and their mutual relationships. Genes and memes are transmitted only through specific manifest behaviors and through specific psychic processes connected to such behaviors. Furthermore, the influence of biology on culture (as in the cases described by sociobiology) or of culture on biology, still has to be mediated by concrete psychological acts. For instance, giving up a job in order to be able to take care of children (biology *versus* culture) or, on the other hand, choosing to use artifacts noxious to physical health, such as a cigarette or a lethal weapon (culture *versus* biology), both represent instances of psychic functioning.

This centrality of psychic mechanisms with respect to the development of biological and cultural processes (and their respective teleonomies) can also be further extended. Such an extension will lead to the definition of a specifically psychological teleonomy. As we have seen, several clues indicate the tendency to an invariant replication of certain psychic states and processes. We shall proceed in this direction, taking into closer consideration that the theoretical examples reported up to this point – as cases of teleonomic regularity and repetition – do not sufficiently evidence the presence of self-generative processes of internal states and therefore share the risk of mechanistic reductionism mentioned in the first section of this chapter. Psychoanalysis and cognitivism essentially hold a homeostatic view of behavior, a view according to which the search for balance and good organization is predetermined by certain rules that, although increasingly more complex (in function of

18

the requirements of the life cycle), do not fully satisfy the negentropic requirement typical of teleonomic projects and the evolution of information.

A further theoretical development is therefore needed in order to examine and reconsider in such light other psychological theories that will be able to better respond to the teleonomic properties; in particular, the tendency towards an increase of order, information, and complexity. We will thus attempt to avoid the mechanistic or reductionistic risks.

1.4 THE SELF AND THE DEVELOPMENT OF BEHAVIOR

We shall now review synthetically some theories commonly linked by the above-mentioned effort toward a theoretical development, with particular attention being paid to the role assigned more or less explicitly to evolving aspects of behavior.

1.4.1 The "Pure Ego" of Popper and Eccles

We shall mention, first of all, the view developed by Popper (1972) and subsequently reconsidered by Eccles (1973), a Nobel Prize winner for medicine. In the debate concerning the relationship between mind and brain, both authors assume a "trialist," that is, interactionist position. This view attempts to go beyond the Cartesian dualism in a nonreductionistic way, without appealing to a monistic approach (which favors the biological aspect). Eccles (Fig. 1.1) divides all existing elements and all experience into three categories, which he calls World 1, World 2, and World 3.

World 1 contains physical objects and states, such as natural, artificial, and biological states. World 2 represents the area of the individuals' states of consciousness. World 3 contains knowledge in an objective sense, ideas, and intellectual products: This is the world of culture.

The three worlds continuously interact and depend on one another. For instance, a philosophical conception (World 3) has to

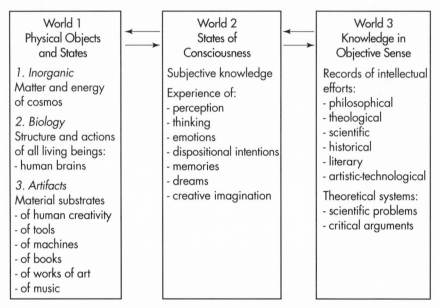

World 1 Physical Objects and States	World 2 States of Consciousness	World 3 Knowledge in Objective Sense
1. *Inorganic* Matter and energy of cosmos 2. *Biology* Structure and actions of all living beings: - human brains 3. *Artifacts* Material substrates - of human creativity - of tools - of machines - of books - of works of art - of music	Subjective knowledge Experience of: - perception - thinking - emotions - dispositional intentions - memories - dreams - creative imagination	Records of intellectual efforts: - philosophical - theological - scientific - historical - literary - artistic-technological Theoretical systems: - scientific problems - critical arguments

Figure 1.1. Tabular representation of the three worlds that comprise all existents and all experiences as defined by Popper (in Eccles, 1973, p.189).

be expressed in a code appropriate to the materials contained in World 1 – such as, in our contemporary culture, paper or the magnetic substrate of a computer. Similarly, one can experience that very idea in World 2 only through a complex path moving through World 1, which is to say, by means of the biological system represented by cerebral neurons, which decodes the message and transforms it into subjective states of consciousness. However, it is the activity of World 2 (for instance, cognition or creative imagination) that, through the substrates provided by World 1 (neurons and material substrates in which products of World 2 are deposited), will constitute World 3.

In this complex view, characterized by mutual and circular processes of causation, World 2 constitutes, according to these authors, our primary reality. This world is also viewed as a composite and dynamic structure.

According to Eccles (1973), there is a first level, outer sense, constituted by common sensation provided by sensory organs. These qualities are not present in World 1, in which instead chemical substances or electromagnetic waves are found. There is then a second level, inner sense, constituted by more subtle sensations deriving from the internal world. This is the area of emotions, memories, imagination, and plans for the future. Finally, at the center, contained within these other two levels, there is the essence of an individual or the *"pure ego,* which is the basis of our unity as an experiencing being throughout our whole lifetime" (Eccles, 1973, p.191). This definition reunites two fundamental elements. First of all, the unity is central in that it is conscious. Consciousness is here formed through an integration of internal and external stimuli.

This integration is an original act belonging exclusively to a single individual. We shall come back to this notion at a later time, as it is an important one along our theoretical journey. Furthermore, this central component of the individual is not thought of as static. Rather, as we have seen, World 2 continuously interacts with the other two Worlds. In particular, World 2 constantly receives information from World 3, information that World 2 then decodes, elaborates, and gives back to the environment by means of linguistic and behavioral acts. World 2, the "pure ego," is continuously modified while preserving itself as a unity: just as bony tissue retains its internal structure, despite constant modification by deconstruction and rebuilding, in the same way the core of an individual remains intact and constant, according to Eccles, thanks to the continuous relational dynamic activity present between parts existing within the individual and parts existing in external reality.

1.4.2 Personality and the Formation of the Ego According to Non-Western Cultures

We shall now proceed to consider an idea proposed by Sow (1977), one of the best-known African psychiatrists. Once more it will be possible for the reader to notice the thread that connects (1) the

21

concepts exposed at the beginning of the chapter, (2) the thought of Popper and Eccles, and (3) the thought of Sow.

Sow's thought has been reconsidered and partially modified by Terranova-Cecchini (1991), who also points out the way in which his ideas are valid for many other traditional cultures. According to Sow, the Ego consists of three parts, rightly connected both mutually and to the external world.

The nucleus, the so-called "substance of the Ego," is an ancestral substance. It represents the incorporation (or introjection) by the Ego of traditions, of the fundamental laws of the community, and of spiritual and religious values. This central part forms a vertical connection with the basis of the culture to which one belongs, and therefore allows joining the personality with the structural forces shared by the community. This central part can be thought of as being contained in an area of the personality defined by Sow as the *vital force*, deriving from ties to the family, considered in both its biological and cultural aspects. This part of the Ego therefore contains the direct genetic and memic inheritance and builds itself through its daily ties to the members of the family, both nuclear and extended.

There is also a more external part of the Ego, connected to the bodily envelope, which is tied to the more extended social relations and is in contact with the external environment, both material and natural. It represents that part of the identity that is developed by belonging to different real groups and by the interiorization of the groups' respective norms and values.

Although Sow's thought is derived from entirely different bases and traditions, here we approach the concept of social identity proposed by Tajfel (1981): the fundamental sense of belonging to a group and of personal enhancement that derives from being in contact with the social world. The individual is considered as a biocultural entity that forms itself through the conjunction of cultural, biological, social, and material memories.

But the formation of the self is achieved in an open fashion. Through a continuous relationship with immaterial contexts (tradition, values, social relations) and material contexts (environmental artifacts, means of subsistence), and on the basis of a specific biological foundation, the individual is able to maintain the connection with his or her biocultural traditions and, strengthened by this security, is at the same time able to develop original ways of organizing experience and new behavioral strategies. Health and sickness, development or restraint of behavior, derive from an integrated[2] relationship between the different levels of the personality and the different axes connecting the individual to the external world.

This approach (which in Sow's elaboration, here only sketched, is more complex in that the model assumes different forms for matrilineal and patrilineal societies) can easily be connected to the view of the world held by a great majority of non-Western societies. Furthermore, it confirms the possibility of an evolutionary conception of the individual's structure in a mutually determining relationship with external contexts. This view questions the notion of a person as solely an individual entity, separated from the community to which it belongs. Yet, such a view has prevailed throughout history and has lead to viewing the description and understanding of the individual's uniqueness as the principal nucleus of personality psychology.

In this regard, Berry, Poortinga, Segal and Dasen (1992) report a series of rigorous research data, the most significant of which are reported here. Shweder and Bourne (1984), on the basis of research done in the Indian state of Orissa, point out that the personality is modified in function of external relationships and has to be described in terms of social relations, not in terms of stable traits. Similarly, Marsella, De Vos and Hsu (1985) point out the relationship between the conception of the person and individualistic and collective dimensions in Asian and Western cultures.

Cross-cultural research, starting from anthropological explorations of personality (Burridge, 1979; Carrithers, Collins and Luckes, 1985) and from anthropological considerations regarding the Ego (Miller, 1988), tends to bridge the separation between personality psychology and social psychology (Yang and Bond, 1990). This objective is shared by authoritative exponents of personality psychology (Krahé, 1992).

Triandis (1989), after having reviewed several studies, shows that the more a culture is individualistic, the more frequently its components focus their attention on factors and information regarding the Ego, understood as a separate entity. On the other hand, cultures with collective characteristics think of the individual as a complex entity, and consequently their members tend to overvalue the social aspects of the personality.

These studies point out the increasing necessity to widen the typically Western conception of the Ego, which considers the individual as a separate, autonomous, and atomized entity, which therefore tries to be separate and independent from others. To the contrary – as it is suggested by traditional cultures showing the importance of connection, interdependence, and relationships – the Ego has to be understood as a discrete entity, but intrinsically connected to others. A person finds his or her identity and meaning only within his or her position in a complex society, while at the same time maintaining autonomy and specificity (Berry, Poortinga, Segall and Dasen, 1992).

The view that focuses on the centrality of the autonomy of the self and its evolving aspects, in connection with the contexts of life, finds its roots in the history of psychological disciplines. In this sense, it is useful to introduce into our discussion, even if only briefly, the thought of George H. Mead.

1.4.3 The I and the Me in the Thought of George H. Mead

Mead made a significant contribution in the domain of the behavioral sciences in general. His conception of psychic development and the formation of the self goes beyond the discipline of social psychology within which Mead is usually located, to assume the connotations of a general theory of individual and social development. The importance granted to the evolving and self-determining aspects, and to the mutually influencing relationship between internal world and social context, brings his work within the context of our discussion.

Mead never systematically formalized his thought. He developed his ideas while teaching a very successful course in social psychology for several years, which trained a whole generation of scholars, starting in 1900, at The University of Chicago. Mead's classes, rich in arguments and theoretical contributions, were always delivered without written notes. It was his students who finally collected Mead's thought in the widely known publication *Mind, Self and Society* (1934).

Mead's fundamental project was to show that the mind and the self emerge from social interaction, and these, in turn, allow social organization to arise. We shall now briefly expose the main aspects of Mead's theories.

The mind is understood as an entity constituted by meaningful symbols. It derives from the individual's internalization of the social process of communication. The starting point is not the individual mind but the objective social process. The latter is coded by language and decoded by the individual who in this way incorporates the social act. This, therefore, is the social aspect of the mind: a thought advances by means of the subject's assimilation of others' roles, and by means of controlling his or her own behavior on the basis of this assimilation of roles. It is because of language and the use of its symbols that we can assimilate others' roles and we can thus observe ourselves from this external perspective and hence become an object to ourselves. This capacity of an organism endowed with a mind to become an object to him or herself is, according to Mead, what makes the development of the self possible. This self is an entity different from the biological organism and is able to become self-conscious.

According to Mead, there are two stages in the development of the self: the stage of play, and the stage of the game.

> In play the child simply assumes one role after another of persons and animals that have in some way or other entered into its life. . . In the game, however, one has become, as it were, all of the others implicated in the common activity – must have within one's self the whole organized activity in order to successfully play one's own part. The person here has not merely assumed

the role of a specific other, but of any other participating in the common activity; he has generalized the attitude of role-taking (Mead, 1934, p.xxiv).

Thus, the subject takes on the attitude or role of the "generalized other."

Through a social process, therefore, the biological individual achieves a mind and a self:

> In virtue of the internalization or importation of the social process of communication, the individual gains the mechanism of reflective thought (the ability to direct his action in terms of the foreseen consequences of alternatives courses of action); acquires the ability to make himself an object to himself and to live in a common moral and scientific world; [. . .] (*ibid.*, p.xxv-xxvi).

According to Mead, other people's attitudes, as specific or generalized as they may be, once internalized in the self, will constitute the "Me." The Me is that part of the self that can be observed as an object and that can be described by the subject.

Thus, owing to the progressive development of the social network and the consequent taking on of roles, this part of the self, the Me, becomes increasingly rich and complex. However, if the subjective part of the individual were formed exclusively by this reflection of the social structure, we could not distinguish the different parts, and we would a priori exclude the possibility of any creative and reconstructive activity. Mead avoids this reductionistic risk by pointing out a second component of the self, the "I."

> The "I" is the principle of action and of impulse; and in its action it changes the social structure. . . . "[T]he individual is no thrall of society. He constitutes society as genuinely as society constitutes the individual" (*ibid.*, p.xxv).

The function of this part of the self is not only to innovate the social context, but also to procure new material for the formation of the entire self. In this regard, Mead's words are enlightening:

[The "I"] is the answer which the individual makes to the attitude which others take toward him when he assumes an attitude toward them. Now, the attitudes he is taking toward them are present in his own experience, but his response to them will contain a novel element. The "I" gives the sense of freedom, of initiative. The situation is there for us to act in a self-conscious fashion. We are aware of ourselves, and of what the situation is, but exactly how we will act never gets into experience until after the action takes place (*ibid.*, 177–178).

The I is not experienced in the same way as the Me. The latter represents something like a schema that the community offers to our attitudes and that is ready to procure coherent and organized answers. Owing to the function of the I, such answers are not predetermined. Consequently, there is the necessity, not for a mechanical, but, in Mead's terminology, for a moral action – which is to say, aiming at coherence and organization.

The action of the I seems to fully carry out functions connected with a teleonomic project of the psychic world: self-organization, psychic negentropy, and increase of order and complexity, all based on the interconnection of Me and I. The latter are separated in this process but they penetrate each other, they are part of a same whole, the one having organizational and integrative functions, the other having emergent functions and functions related to presenting new information to the psychic world.

Mead tells us that Me requires a specific I in order to face the demands of the external world, but the I is always something different from what the situation requires. The I can never be perfectly determined.

The "I" both calls out the "me" and responds to it. Taken together they constitute a personality as it appears in social experience. The self is essentially a social process going on with these two distinguishable phases. If it did not have these two phases there could not be conscious responsibility, and there would be nothing novel in experience (*ibid.*, p.178).

Mead insists on a bivalence of the self. On the one hand, the self is the mirror of the organized social structure, and insofar as it is

27

so it allows the individual to communicate and relate to others. On the other hand, the self is an unrepeatable, unique, and developing entity. This uniqueness allows for the gradual change of the social structure.

In order to connect these two factors, sameness and change, the author introduces the concept of experience:

> As I have pointed out, the ego or "I" that is responsible for changes of the sort appears in experience only after its reaction has taken place. It is only after we have said the word we are saying that we recognize ourselves as the person that has said it, as this particular self that says this particular thing; it is only after we have done the thing that we are going to do that we are aware of what we are doing. However carefully we plan the future it always is different from that which we can previse, and this something that we are continually bringing in and adding to is what we identify with the self that comes into the level of our experience only in the completion of the act (*ibid.*, p.203).

The vital action of the I never enters into the mediated experience. It is free experience. It only has to face action while it occurs. For Mead, the action of the I is tied to psychic energies that lie beyond immediate consciousness. This disengagement of consciousness allows for the development of the innovative aspect of the self. The latter, on the other hand, is always under the influence of the social reality through the functions of the Me. The self develops through experience and allows the external contexts to change. In this respect, Mead speaks of the social creativity of the emergent self.

However, the innovative contribution of the I is not necessarily positive: It can either consist in a process leading to the degeneration of the social situation or, to the contrary, to a greater internal integration of it. Mead uses the example of the crowd, which allows for original parts of self to come forward. However, if the latter are not restrained by an organized social structure (the crowd itself not being so), they can lead to a degeneration of the context. This view indicates that the increased complexity of a system (either social or individual), which is to say, the evolution of the information contained in it, is from a moral point of view neutral, since what is new and more complex is not good or bad *per se*, but only richer in information. This is a concept proper to evolutionary theories which, beginning with Darwin, point out that "more evolved" does not necessarily mean better, but only more adaptive to a given environment (Barash, 1977).

Going back to Mead, we shall mention that the relationship between the Me, I, and social reality evolves, according to this author, due to a mechanism of mutually determining processes according to which each element is continuously influenced by the others. The innovative role of certain functions of the self, the concept of emergent experience, the principle of mutually determining processes, and the neutrality of the increase in complexity – from the point of view of social morality and norm – are all concepts that will be reconsidered in following chapters. They are also in harmony with some more recent theoretical principles reviewed in the preceding sections. Mead's thought is therefore still stimulating for the ongoing discussions in many areas of the psychological sciences.

1.5 THE INDIVIDUAL AND SOCIETY

Since the 1930s, Mead was focusing his attention on the existence (within general psychology, and social psychology in particular) of two fundamental and opposed points of view. They can be defined respectively as social and individual theories concerning the interaction of individual and culture. Generally speaking, the former represents the self as deriving from social processes and from the relationships in which the self is involved, and with which it empirically interacts, thus producing experiences. The latter represents social processes as deriving from the selves of the individuals involved in these processes. In the second case, the individuals, understood as separate entities, are deemed to be the logical and biological presuppositions of the social process and order with which they interact. These conceptions reflect, as previously mentioned, two antithetical modes of thinking, one belonging to traditional and non-Western cultures, the other to the Western world. Theoretical debates within psychology, and in particular within social psychology, still focus on these two antithetical positions (Amerio, 1982; Ugazio, 1988; Palmonari, 1989).

The first position is represented by several European thinkers, such as H. Tajfel (1981, 1982). His fundamental claims can be summarized as follows:

- Integration between an interactionist and constructivist approach
- Study of social interaction and of how, through such interaction, social and individual processes are formed
- Appraisal of an individual as an active subject that represents the environment to itself and does not merely react to it; the individual orders reality on the basis of his or her culture and the ideologies of the group to which he or she belongs
- Interest in studying systematic variations of these ordering processes
- Interest not so much in specific individual cognitive functions, as in "large" cognitive structures: representations, systems of belief, implicit theories
- Interest in studying real-life behaviors: in addition to laboratory research, quasi-experimental research plans and observational and descriptive methods are developed

The second theoretical approach focuses on the individual and is nowadays well represented, for instance, by the most traditional cognitive sciences. Its fundamental claims are:

- Individualistic perspective: the subject can be studied and understood out of context and independently from social interaction
- Naive and ahistorical conception of society, considered (substantially) as a simple set of single individuals
- Appraisal of a subject as an elaborator of information and an optimizer of cognitive resources

- Appraisal of social objects as inanimate objects, lacking structuring or generative functions
- Search for maximum methodological precision, in an objective and quantitative sense: primacy of experimental studies carried out in laboratories

Among the first approach, the view developed by Serge Moscovici (by means of a sophisticated theoretical, methodological, and research commitment) is particularly relevant and important.

The complex thought of Moscovici (1961–76, 1969, 1981, 1984) can be mentioned here only in its essential principles. First of all, this author rejects behaviorism, especially as far as the separation and contraposition between an experiencing subject and the external world is concerned. Moscovici, in fact, claims that subject and object are essentially not separate. To represent something to oneself implies that at that moment stimulus and response are found together, undifferentiated (Moscovici, 1973).

The cognitivist point of view is also considered reductionist. Human beings are not simple elaborators of information, but are active subjects able to build their own internal and external reality. This constructivist aspect brings Moscovici to reject, from another perspective, views that take into consideration the structuring function of social life, which he deems too rigid and static. Among these, we can mention for instance Durkheim's concept of collective representations (1895), which, according to Moscovici, hardly takes into consideration the active role of the subject, since collective representations are, in a sense, "given" to the latter, and since the margin within which the subject can transform them actively, with his or her mental processes, is limited. On this basis, Moscovici defines in an original way (1961–76) the idea of social representation.

What precisely are social representations? In order to answer this question we shall make use of brief definitions that are, nevertheless, rich in meaning, starting with the ones offered by Moscovici himself.

1. "By social representations, we mean a set of concepts, statements and explanations originating in daily life in the course

of inter-individual communications." (Moscovici, 1981, p.181) "Social representations are phenomena that are linked with a special way of acquiring and communicating knowledge, a way that creates realities and common sense" (*ibid.*, p.186).

2. "[S]ocial representations are cognitive systems with a logic and language of their own. . . . [A] social representation is a system of values, ideas and practices with a twofold function; first, to establish an order which will enable individuals to orientate themselves in their material and social world and to master it; and secondly to enable communication to take place among the members of a community by providing them with a code for social exchange and a code for naming and classifying unambiguously the various aspects of their world and their individual and group history" (Moscovici, 1973, p.xiii).

3. "Social representations are specific ways of knowing given by the object reflecting itself in the activity of the subject; therefore, they hold a particular position: they stand between a concept, which aims at extracting what is real, and an image, which reproduces the real in a meaningful way" (Palmonari, 1980, p.228).

4. The five fundamental characters of social representation are the following (Jodelet, 1984): it is always the representation of an object; it is rich in images, and it has the property of making the material and the idea, the perception and the concept, interchangeable; it is symbolic and meaningful; it is constructive; it is autonomous and creative.

Starting from these definitions, one might better understand the concept of social representation by analyzing the reasons and the aims for which they are formed. For this reason it might be useful to proceed by exclusion: We can observe that in the formation of social representations, according to Moscovici, the principal mechanisms proposed by the most established psychological theories are not active. In fact, we do not form social representations in the interest of psychic economy. They are not a pure subjective distortion of reality, developed for cognitive or affective purposes. They are not developed in order to compensate an unbalance, and they do not derive from affective tensions due to a lack of integration with reality and other human beings. And finally, they are not formed in order to have cognitive control, meaning they do not filter incoming information. Rather, the subject forms social representations in order to transform the foreign into the familiar, in order to adapt the unknown to known categories and in order to build internally what was once external.

An individual faced with something new coming from the external context rebuilds it internally on the basis of information already present in the internal world (because of past experiences) and in a way suitable for communicating with the members of the group to which he or she belongs. For instance, the current increase in immigration brings many of us to confront ourselves, in the course of our daily lives, with points of view, customs, fashions, and mechanisms of social or familial interaction different from our own. The latter are regulated by categories and signs familiar to us, which are consolidated and connected with our sense of identity. The comparison with, and often the contraposition to, the "other," to difference, makes us react cognitively and emotionally: dissonance, incomprehension, stereotypes (all cognitive factors) are accompanied by prejudices, emotional reactions, and the possibility of feeling attacked in the security derived from our identity, and also in the control of our environment and resources (factors related to relationships, affects, and actions).

Faced with this situation, and all others that imply a contact with new conceptual systems (from a foreign culture to a new fashion), we react by forming a social representation. This is achieved by means of two principal mechanisms: anchoring and objectification. *Anchoring* is a process of incorporating what is foreign in our web of categories. To anchor in fact means to classify and name. By means of this mechanism we rebuild our perception of what is new, adapting it to familiar concepts. Along this line, we can use the example of the association (developed in the collective imagination when psychoanalysis became widespread in nonspecialized domains in both France and Italy) of the image of the

33

psychoanalyst with the image of a confessor, which is a far more familiar image in the Catholic culture proper to those countries.

The second process is *objectification*, which is to say, the transformation of an abstract concept present in our thoughts into something almost concrete present in "nature." The foreign therefore acquires a realistic quality – being part of the known and tangible reality – thus becoming controllable.

Both mechanisms balance, and at the same time transform, external reality. The new, coming from the social world, is partially transformed and connected to the categories of the internal world. These categories contribute to create a sense of personal identity. On the other hand, the shared and subjective (that is to say social and individual at the same time) new knowledge then becomes rooted in what is real. The latter is thus transformed, by means of the daily cognitions and behaviors of social groups. We can therefore see how social representations can be well integrated into the current of thought that rejects mechanistic and homeostatic views of behavior. The constructive activity of the subject, who transforms social data and then places them once again in the external context, points out the possibility for the human mind to generate information (negentropic possibility). This capacity is supported by the possibility for self-determination of the subject. In this light, social representations constitute another important step in our endeavor, which aims at pointing out the evolving aspects of behavior. In the following chapter, we shall enter the core of this issue.

2

THEORIES OF SUBJECTIVE EXPERIENCE AND THE DEVELOPMENT OF PERSONALITY

A T THE END OF THE THIRD SECTION OF THE PRECEDING chapter, we pointed out how the major schools of psychology – psychoanalysis, behaviorism, and cognitivism – presented some of the characteristics of teleonomic projects, meaning the repetition of constant factors and regularities. Furthermore, we showed how these psychological schools do not fully satisfy the teleonomic requirements, in that they tend not to express in their paradigms the possibility for autonomous morphogenesis, which is to say, the capacity for the self-generation of negentropic psychic states.

To the contrary, these schools emphasize homeostatic and mechanistic aspects of the psyche. For this very reason, such theories, at least as they present themselves to date, do not seem to be fully suited to satisfy the fundamental function of psychic processes as proposed and highlighted in the introductory sections of this volume. Once again, such a function consists in the regular replication of specific psychic states and, at the same time, in an ordered and self-determined evolution of the complexity of information contained in these same psychic processes, or connected to them. Fulfilling such tasks, psychological teleonomy becomes, as we have seen, the bridge between biological and cultural processes.

The theories presented in the last sections of the first chapter share instead a number of aspects that tend to better satisfy the teleonomic requirements concerning the increase of complexity.

Authors such as Eccles, Sow, Mead, and Moscovici, even if in many ways quite different from one another, are all part of a general position according to which internal states and social contexts, internalized and externalized culture, are viewed as standing in a mutually dependent, causal relation: psychic processes and individual behaviors both influence and are influenced by the evolving dynamics of culture. This dynamic and active process allows for the evolution of complexity, order, and information (which are typical negentropic characteristics) of both systems under investigation – i.e., the individual and the social.

From a careful analysis of these authors, which provide us with a model for a more general theoretical approach, the reader will be able to identify as an ulterior common trait a certain theoretical deficiency. These different theories point out the interactive process between cultural memory and individual development, thus highlighting the evolving and self-determining quality of internal states and social behavior. However, they do not dwell as much on the specific modalities through which this interaction and development, both at the level of subjective experience and daily life, take place. It follows that they do not emphasize the presence of *experiential* regularities and their replication (which are the primary elements of teleonomic processes) in the interaction between the individual and its contexts, nor is it taken to be their first priority.

Let us take into consideration, for instance, the continuous relationship between Eccles's World 1, World 2, and World 3: Which are the experiential conditions in virtue of which this integration takes place cohesively and prevents a destructive break from occurring between the three Worlds? According to Sow, the vertical tie with tradition and the horizontal tie with the family and the community are the elements promoting the development of the self and the transmission of a culture over time. But which internal processes, which kinds of experiential factors, support such ties? Mead clearly highlights the relationship between the self, its components, and society, but what is the actual experience of the self when it interacts with the social environment? Moscovici skillfully shows the psychosocial mechanism of the formation and function of social representations, but, once again, what is the experience of individuals when they form a representation and share it with the other members of their group? In other words, is the quality of the experience connected with Moscovici's anchoring and objectification processes secondary, preceding, or perhaps even the causal agent by virtue of which such processes become activated, therefore leading to the formation of social representations?

Overall, these questions suggest that the theories under investigation (i.e., Eccles, Sow, Mead, Moscovici) privilege the evolving aspects of behavior, overcoming in this way one of the limits of the homeostatic and mechanistic schools. Yet, they do not sufficiently highlight the importance of the tendency of replication of internal states. This element remains implicit, as we have seen, among the current group of theories. We are therefore faced with a deficiency: the fundamental aspects of a teleonomic project – namely, the replication of a content of invariance and the increase in complexity of information – are not both present.

From another angle, we have seen that it is possible to speak of psychological teleonomy, and that this teleonomy once again plays a central role in the basic processes of human biological and cultural evolution. It is therefore necessary to consider from this vantage other theoretical issues, once already developed by the behavioral sciences, which may better satisfy the requirements of psychological teleonomy.

2.1 SELECTION

To this end, it is useful to analyze a concept that will be crucial to our discussion: the concept of selection. The selection of external and internal information has always been of interest to psychology. The classical literature on the selective function of attention (Miller, 1956; Kahneman, 1973; Keele, 1973; Csikzentmihalyi, 1978a) comes to mind. But it was actually William James, one of the founding fathers of the discipline of psychology, who strongly emphasized this subject. In his *Principles of Psychology* (1890), in the chapter on the so-called "stream of thought," James writes:

[*Consciousness*] *is always interested more in one part of its object than in another, and welcomes and rejects, or chooses, all the while it thinks.* The phenomena of selective attention and of deliberative will are of course patent examples of this choosing activity. But few of us are aware how incessantly it is at work in operations not ordinarily called by these names. Accentuation and Emphasis are present in every perception we have (Vol. I, p.284).

And again:

. . . the mind is at every stage a theater of simultaneous possibilities. Consciousness consists in the comparison of these with each other, the selection of some, and the suppression of the rest by the reinforcing and inhibiting agency of attention (*ibid.,* p.288).

Later we shall come back in greater detail to the relationship between attention and consciousness and shall consider some relevant psychoanalytic concepts, such as evenly suspended attention (Freud, 1900). Let us now turn, however, to examine another domain in which the concept of selection is crucial: the evolutionary theory of Darwin (1859).

As Barash mentions (1977), Darwin's theory is founded on the concept of selection. From (1) the tendency of organisms to over-reproduce, (2) the tendency of populations of organisms to remain relatively numerically stable, and from (3) the fact that all organisms (barring identical twins) differ from one another, follows the competition among organisms in which some succeed to survive and reproduce more than others. This is what makes up natural selection. Acting on individual differences, it brings about a gradual change in the characteristics of a population, which, in turn, leads to natural evolution.

Darwinian theories are of particular interest for psychology, not only from the point of view of evolutionary psychology (Barkow, 1991) which emphasizes the biological bases and the origin of psychic processes in connection with their adaptive advantages for survival, but also because of their general theoretical implications. Darwin (1859) makes a connection between the concept of selection and the concept of accumulation of information in memory (Darwin was talking about biological information, but in the psychological sciences we can also talk about cultural or internal information). He also specifies that selection is not to be thought of simply as a phenomenon of choice.

The distinction between these two terms, choice and selection, is also well underlined by their respective definition in the Italian language. Although "choice" [It: *scelta*] simply consists in "taking from several items the most suited, best, or most liked one" (Palazzi, 1939), "selection" [It: *selezione*] is defined as that "choice made by rejecting or preserving" (*ibid.*), which implies the possibility of accumulating the selected information.

Furthermore, this definition can also be integrated with modern conceptions concerning storage of information (Massimini, 1993) – according to which the concept of selection is far more complex than the concept of choice, since only the former implies the introduction of new information into memory – meaning stored information accumulated *via* preceding selections. More specifically, we can mention the principles of conservation of information proposed by Massimini (1993) (while also taking into consideration a large literature review on the subject). These principles account for all types of information: at the biological level stored in cellular chromosomes, at the cultural level in human artifacts, and at the psychic level, once internalized, in the central nervous system. The full understanding of these principles will be achieved when considering the equivalence of information and negative entropy, as already shown.

The first principle was offered by Volkenstein and Chernavskii (1978). It claims:

> The evolution of the Universe, biological evolution as a specific expression of the evolution of the Universe, the ontogenetic development of a living organism and the creative activity of man mean the creation of new information (ibid., p.95).

This means that the above phenomena are characterized by a certain amount of instability and disorder by which (by selecting from different possibilities) organisms and artifacts arrive at progressive states of stability and order that will contain new information in the full negentropic sense.

The second principle, which also goes back to Volkenstein and Chernavskii (1978) and Pattee (1973), claims that the creation of new information resulting from previous instability is irreversible. Evolution, regardless of the system of information it refers to, never retraces its own steps: an adult can never be retransformed into an embryo; the words composing the ten commandments in the Bible can never return to an undifferentiated state, because their meaning is stored in the cultural memory of humanity.

The third principle, tied elliptically to the preceding ones, claims that the creation of new information corresponds to the memory of a choice. Such memory consists in the irreversible shift from an unstable state, where choice is still possible, to a stable state, where choices have already been made. In this way, we can speak of selection of information (Massimini, 1993).

The fourth principle claims that, regardless of the means of communication being used, a previously memorized bit of information will influence the reception and the selection of new, incoming information. This is congruent with the mechanisms of the so-called anticipatory systems operating within both biological and social systems (Rosen, 1978; Massimini, 1993). Memory is therefore an organized system that regulates, by selection, new information to be memorized by way of a feedback mechanism. In this manner, open systems, although continuously exchanging energy and information with the environment (Miller, 1970), ensure for themselves a state of dynamic order.

These principles are also related to the concept of "autopoiesis" – meaning the self-generating capacity of all living systems – which has been more recently elaborated by scholars such as Maturana and Varela (1980; for an overview of their work see Calegari, 1992). In particular, we can mention one of the main properties of autopoietic systems according to these authors, namely, autonomy. By *autonomy* we mean a condition in which all changes are subordinated to the preservation of organization.

Here we are referring to the capacity of systems (understood as finite sets of elements) to maintain their identity by actively adjusting to changes and incoming information.

We therefore have available to us a series of concepts that add to the general theoretical considerations developed in the introductory sections. The concept of selection and the principles of storage of information in a system of organized memory (such as the human mind) complete the requirements that a theory of psychic functioning must meet in order to be teleonomic. We now have to identify theories that will be able to describe psychic processes and organizations of the mental apparatus as having the following characteristics:

1. Replicated regularities are present within psychic functioning.
2. These organizations or regular psychic processes have the capacity to actively integrate new information.
3. Information comes from the external world, which is selected because of its congruence with the accumulated memory (represented by the repetition of regularities), and at the same time because it brings new order and differentiation.
4. Information comes from within psychic organization and processes thanks to their capacity for self-generation; this new self-determined and self-produced information is selected for the same reasons as in the previous point, which is to say, because it is compatible with the information already accumulated in memory (the regularities), and at the same time because it brings new order and differentiation.

Before proceeding to the analysis of theories that satisfy these requirements, it is also necessary to briefly take into consideration another theoretical issue. We are referring to a central problem for many branches of the psychological sciences and, in particular, for cognitive psychology: the relationship between consciousness and attention. We shall not consider the issue in all its breadth and complexity; once more, we shall expose synthetically only those parts necessary for this theoretical investigation.

41

2.2 CONSCIOUSNESS AND ATTENTION

In *The Encyclopedic Dictionary of Psychology* (Harré, Lamb and Mecacci, 1986) we read the following definition of consciousness:

(a) the state of an individual animal is alert and capable of action, contrasted with unconsciousness
(b) the quality that an animal species has of being capable of being aware or conscious of objects in the environment [. . .]
(c) the state of being aware of some of one's thoughts, perceptions or emotions, also known as self-consciousness
(d) the capacity of human beings to have an organized mental life, in which each individual's experience has a particular perceived quality
(e) the system of states of mind which organize and coordinate thoughts and actions, contrasted with subconscious (p.114).

The definition given by the various biocultural theories (see, Inghilleri, 1993a) is particularly useful. According to these theories, consciousness is the locus where the information coming from the environment (extrasomatic cultural instructions) interacts with the information coming from an individual's internal world (genetic and cultural intrasomatic instructions). Consciousness, according to this definition, is therefore the locus where the subjective experiences of human beings are deposited and developed.

At the same time, the great majority of theories connects consciousness with the function of attention, in particular with *selective* attention. In fact, several authors hold the role of attention to be central in the regulation of states of consciousness. James, for instance, claimed that

Millions of items of the outward order are present to my senses which never properly enter into my experience. Why? Because they have no *interest* for me. *My experience is what I agree to attend*

42

to. Only those items which I *notice* shape my mind – without selective interest, experience is an utter chaos (James, 1890, Vol. II, p.402).

James defines the process of attention in a way that it is still valid, relating it to the concept of selection, understood as previously defined:

> Every one knows what attention is. It is the taking possession by the mind, in clear and vivid form, of one out of what seem several simultaneously possible objects or trains of thought. Focalization, concentration, of consciousness are of its essence. It implies withdrawal from some things in order to deal effectively with others, [. . .] (*ibid.*, pp.403–4).

Since the 1950s, with the development of cognitivism, there have been many studies on attention, the great majority of which were concerned with its selective aspects and with its relation to memory and consciousness (among many, we note the studies of Cherry, 1953; Miller, 1956; Broadbent, 1958; Neisser, 1967; Norman, 1969).

Several selective mechanisms have been proposed: some focus on the characteristics of stimuli that could be filtered through attention (Broadbent, 1958); others moved the mechanism of selection to a more complex and earlier level, hypothesizing that each incoming signal finds its proxy in memory, and in this way acquires its meaning, which will consequently determine its selection or exclusion (Norman, 1969). In this model, memory is brought into relation with incoming information, although in a mechanistic fashion. Generally speaking, the idea that attention is a finite resource has been established – although its limitations are not understood along the lines of a "hydraulic" model (characteristic of nineteenth century physics), meaning, as a reservoir with limited capacity that may be exhausted. Limitations of attention are to be understood in a dynamic sense, based on the fact that few units of information, or bits, can be processed in a given unit of time.

In 1956 Miller summarized the research concerning the analysis of human information, emphasizing the concept of capacity, and showing that human organisms have a limit of selection consisting of seven bits of information per unit of time (by bit we understand the quantity of information necessary to take a decision when faced with two equivalent alternatives [Norman, 1969]). The studies on the relationship between consciousness and attention have been reviewed by Csikzentmihalyi (1988b). His critical analysis presents material well-known to cognitive psychologists, while introducing additional interesting theoretical contributions.

Csikzentmihalyi, recasting and to some extent making more specific Dawkins thought (1976, 1982), points out that the biological evolution of the central nervous system brought human beings to develop a complex system of information capable of selecting, storing, and elaborating selectively external and internal stimuli. Such a system is defined as consciousness, and it is constituted by three functional subsystems: *attention,* which selects available information; *awareness,* which interprets information; and *memory,* which stores information.

1. *Attention* is a selective function with a limited capacity that introduces data into consciousness. Therefore, it can also be defined as psychic energy (Kahneman, 1973; Csikzentmihalyi, 1978a).

2. The term *awareness* stands for all those processes that participate in consciousness after a bit of information has been selected. These processes are of three types (Hilgard, 1980): cognition, which includes recognition of the information selected by attention, its categorization in terms of the already available information, and its memorization or abandonment; the emotional component of awareness which defines the affective connotation of the processed information; volition, meaning the process through which attention either stays focused on a given bit of information or turns to other elements.

   In order for all these processes to be operationalized, they in turn require psychic energy, that is, attention, and are therefore subjected to the same limitation of this function. We therefore cannot think, or feel emotion and volition, with respect to an unlimited number of objects per unit of time (Treisman and Gelade, 1980; Treisman and Schmidt, 1982; Hoffman, Nelson and Houck, 1983).

3. The third functional subsystem is *memory*, which stores information. The latter, once stored, can then be recalled. The storage and recall of information also require psychic energy and are therefore subjected to the limitations imposed by the characteristics of attention (Neisser, Hirst and Spelke, 1981).

According to Csikzentmihalyi (1988b), attention, awareness, and memory are functional subsystems of consciousness, whose action forms the content of consciousness itself, which will then constitute subjective experience. The latter can be defined as the sum of all information coming from both the internal and external world, which enters the system at a moment x, and its overall interpretation by awareness. More specifically, experience is understood to be the focus of the attention processes on the interconnections of the data present in consciousness; in other words, it is understood as all the cognitive, motivational, and emotional information capable of producing perceptible modifications (and therefore capable of being selected by attention) in our subjective state (Csikzentmihalyi, 1988b). We shall discuss the concept of subjective experience in more detail at a later time.

It is therefore evident that consciousness is a complex and dynamic system, connected to the selective functions of attention, in which incoming and previous information, cognitive and affective processes, and experiential states are in constant relation. In order to better understand this system, we have to further define the hierarchical relationship between attention and consciousness.

Consciousness and attention have to be considered as two interacting systems, each regulating, and at the same time being regulated by, the other. In particular, consciousness can be thought of as a cybernetic system controlling its own operation by means of attention. Such a system contains information, selected through

45

preceding processes of attention, and guides the process. Attention provides energy to consciousness, and produces new information, derived from both the external and the internal world (Csikzentmihalyi, 1978a, 1988b).

Thus we have a self-regulating relationship between two systems acting in a cybernetic fashion. Hence, there is no hierarchical superiority of consciousness over the attention processes. In other words, on the one hand consciousness points psychic energy toward environmental data (Bagnara, 1984), on the other hand "attention . . . provides energy and new information by introducing unplanned variation into consciousness" (Csikzentmihalyi, 1978a, p.340). Attention can act in a self-determined fashion, on the basis of regulatory instances of the overall system, thus producing "emergent" information (Csikzentmihalyi, 1985).

In relation to this model of the active role of attention, we would like to briefly report some conceptualizations coming from other branches of the behavioral sciences. Within psychoanalytic thought, and in particular its technique, we have mentioned the concept of evenly suspended attention. This is, according to Freud, the

> manner in which . . . the analyst should listen to the analysand: he must give no special, *a priori* importance to any aspect of the subject's discourse; this implies that he should allow his own unconscious activity to operate as freely as possible and suspend the motives which usually direct his attention. This technical recommendation to the analyst complements the rule of free association laid down for the subject being analyzed (Laplanche and Pontalis, 1968, p.43).

Psychoanalytic practice seems to show the possibility of a free and unpredictable flow of attention processes derived from an at least partial suspension of those cognitive elements that usually guide attention – namely, the schemata, biases, personal inclinations, and those ideological principles functioning as points of reference.

Another area to be considered concerns the phenomenology of dreams. Oneiric activity contains, in a sense, cognitive activities: dreams are formed by visual images, emotions, and thought processes (Csikzentmihalyi, 1978a). In a dream, though, consciousness is detached from attention. Individuals have no control over their experiences: the elements experienced in a dream depend on an autonomous focus of the processes of attention on the data contained in the cognitive and affective world of the individual. This spontaneous activation of attention is also pointed out by some of the literature concerned with altered states of consciousness (Tart, 1975; Davinson and Davinson, 1980).

A further contribution is offered by studies of cognitive processes within the domain of schizophrenia (Davinson and Neale, 1986). Among schizophrenics, we often find symptoms such as incoherence of thought (with loss of associative connections) and disturbances in the content of thought. Phenomena such as delirious perception, invasion of thought, and transmission and theft of thought represent instances of deliberate and pathological suspension of attention processes without the possibility of control by consciousness. At times, then, disturbances in the attention processes, with a more or less extended incapacity for active concentration on environmental data, represent the main symptom of schizophrenia (Davinson and Neale, 1986).

These particular phenomena, such as dreams and clinical syndromes, show the capacity of the central nervous system to separate attention and consciousness. Such separation, in these cases, leads to abnormalities, or psychic disorder and disruption. We must now determine whether this separation comes about only in specific situations (as in dreams and pathology), or whether the latter actually reveal a more general physiological mechanism in which the emergent activity of attention is tightly connected to the already present information, and therefore does not lead to disorganization, but to an increase of information, order, and psychic complexity.

Furthermore, the possibility that under given circumstances the data actively and autonomously selected by attention are integrated with the data already present in consciousness, leading to an unforeseen increase in their complexity, is indirectly supported by well-known classical models explaining the functioning of attention. For instance, Neisser (1967), as indicated by Norman

47

(1969), claims that the analysis of incoming information is lead by a preceding analysis of the context and by the expectations present in a given situation. In other words, attention is able to introduce new information into the system, but this new information must have been previously connected with data already present in the system itself. This emergent activity of attention is particularly pertinent to our discussion. For it relates to the general views of behavior already reported, which, on the basis of specific theoretical elements, we have called evolving, negentropic, and non-homeostatic.

The definition of particular conceptual elements (e.g., psychological teleonomy) lead us to point out the need for psychological theories founded on the idea of an information system directed toward order, integration, and at the same time toward an increase of complexity and development (according to the requirements listed in the preceding section). The consciousness-attention system, understood in this way, appears to be useful in that it points out the continuous connection between memorized information (representing regularity and replication) and new incoming information, partially associated with self-generative and emergent functions of attention (representing the increase in complexity).

We shall now direct our attention to two general theories that seem to offer a systematic view that tallies with the considerations developed thus far. The first theory includes the most recent developments of the concept of intrinsic motivation. The second, developed at The University of Chicago, is that of optimal experience or flow.

2.3 INTRINSIC MOTIVATION, EXTRINSIC MOTIVATION, AND SELF-DETERMINATION

2.3.1 Historical Overview

During the 1970s, a new theoretical principle based on an important series of studies infused new life into the field of psychology. Research on intrinsic motivation showed that, under given circumstances, external rewards and material incentives can actually diminish the drive to learn. Furthermore, voluntary learning derived from intrinsic motivation seemed to be rather stable and to become integrated with the identity of the individual. At that time, thanks to this emerging paradigm, the common hope of many researchers was to be able to overcome the reductionist limitations of behaviorism (Condry and Stokker, 1992).

This research stemmed from two complex and long-standing trends in the field: the study of motivation and the study of learning and development. The interest in motivation had been central to two major psychological schools, psychoanalysis (Freud, 1916) and behaviorism (Hull, 1943). These two approaches, though very different from one another, here share a common aspect, namely, the tendency to consider

> that all behavior is basically carried out in an effort to reduce internal tension or stimulation and rests on a limited set of supposedly primary drives, such as those for food, water, and sex (Deci and Ryan, 1980, p.40).

Within this theoretical context, an attempt to resolve this limit was made in psychoanalysis by Ego-psychology (Hartmann, 1958), which focuses on the emergent functions of the Ego, which are partially autonomous from the primary instincts characterizing the other psychic agents.

Within the domain of behaviorism, until the 1970s, not much attention was devoted to emergent aspects of behavior, although authors such as Harlow (1953), Montgomery (1954), and Berlyne (1966) had already observed the tendency of animals to explore new spaces and manipulate unknown objects – which lead them to hypothesize the existence in organisms of an active search for new environmental stimulation, as opposed to a mere response to it. These considerations are to be thought of within the context of the second general line of studies concerning the grounds and meaning of learning and developmental processes.

The thought of Piaget and his school seem to point out an innate tendency toward growth and increase in cognitive and behavioral complexity – not limited to infantile developmental phases, but active along the entire course of life (Piaget, 1954) – which may constitute, for some, the very essence of life, both in a physiological and in a philosophical sense (Piaget, 1971). In other contexts, evolving aspects and the active search for behavior were brought to light by several authors interested in social motivation (McClelland, Atkinson, Clarck and Lowell, 1953) and humanistic psychology (Maslow, 1954).

The central role played by the drive to learn and its relationship with the more stable characteristics of an individual, both from the point of view of cognition and identity, encouraged studies concerned with the basic mechanisms regulating this tendency towards development. Two autonomous groups of theories oriented themselves in this direction.

The first dwells upon the concept of incongruity. According to this group, individuals actively guide their behavior because of the need to find stimuli slightly different with respect to their internal states (as, for instance, with respect to a given cognitive structure) and from the usual environmental stimulation (Hunt, 1965). These concepts are fairly close to Piaget's views on the subject (1954). According to Piaget, individuals search the external environment for slightly different elements in relation to which they can activate accommodation processes. Similarly, Berlyne (1978) observed the tendency of individuals to turn to new situations capable of supplying cognitive elements requiring integration.

The second group of theories is interested in issues regarding self-determination and competence. White (1959) points out that individuals follow their need to feel competent and to be in a position to face environmental demands. According to this author, these needs correspond to an innate motivation to control the environment, which is at the origin of phenomena such as curiosity, exploration games, and some aspects of cognitive development. In particular, this innate motivation explains the autonomous emerging of interest in facing new stimuli and new tasks.

From a different perspective, deCharms (1968) emphasizes the need to perceive oneself as the causal agent of one's own behavior.

According to this author there is an innate drive to experience one-self as active, with respect to the external world, and therefore as self-determined. Within this type of research, due to authors such as Deci and Ryan, founders of the Rochester school, the concept of intrinsic motivation receives its full theoretical elaboration and definition.

2.3.2 Intrinsic Motivation

Internally motivated behaviors are based on the need for competence and self-determination (Deci, 1975). The latter are interconnected and usually covary in real life. Among the two, self-determination seems to be the most fundamental. Without it, the other component would not be able to initiate the process of internal motivation (Deci and Ryan, 1985).

The theoretical construct "intrinsic motivation" has been operationally defined in order to explain those internally motivated behaviors occurring in the absence of any apparent external motivation (Deci and Ryan, 1980). They do not require extrinsic rewards (such as material incentives), but they are rather sustained by internal ones, which is to say, by the spontaneous experience of interest and enjoyment that accompanies them (Deci, 1975). In other words, intrinsically motivated behaviors do not have an instrumental function; it is the experience associated with them which represents their ultimate aim.

Looking at the experimental research on intrinsic motivation, the first fundamental studies were conducted by Deci (1971, 1972). In these studies, as in many that followed after them, subjects were given a puzzle (which is in fact a rather interesting task for students) called Soma. The measure of intrinsic motivation leading to the solution of the puzzle was given by keeping track of the time that a subject would dedicate to the puzzle in a situation in which he could freely choose his or her own activities. In other instances, paper and pencil experiments were also used to measure interest and enjoyment. During the first experiments, the effect of monetary rewards on freely chosen behaviors was observed. The data showed that subjects not offered rewards had the tendency to approach the task, while those offered a monetary reward, once the puzzle had been solved, showed a significant decrease in intrinsic motivation, as compared with subjects in the previous group. This relationship between intrinsic and extrinsic motivation is quite important in this line of research. Its latest developments constitute the central element of our discussion, as we shall see in what follows.

The data gathered lead Deci (1975) to develop the idea of "cognitive evaluation." According to Deci, all behavioral situations, including those that are rewarded, have two properties. On the one hand, there is control, which may be connected with the possible satisfaction of extrinsic needs and with the creation of a hierarchical relationship between rewards and behavior. On the other hand, the situations provide subjects with positive information regarding their competence and efficacy in facing the circumstances. The "control" aspect is connected with extrinsic elements, while the "information" aspect is connected with intrinsic components.

On this basis, following the terminology already employed by Heider (1958) and deCharms (1968), Deci pointed out that the experience of being gratified from the activity itself leads the subject to perceive an internal "locus" of causality (when the information aspect predominates): the subject experiences him or herself as the actor of an adaptive interaction with the environment. Alternately, the presence of external rewards leads to a shift in the perception of the locus of causality, which becomes external to the subject (when the control aspect predominates), leading to a decrease in intrinsic motivation. Several authors associate this phenomenon with a modification of the attributional process (Kruglansky, 1975).

These first studies were followed by a great variety of research and theoretical contributions (Kruglansky, Freedman and Zeevi, 1971; Lepper, Greene and Nisbett, 1973; Ross, 1975; Lepper and Greene, 1978; Deci, 1980; Deci and Ryan, 1980; Ryan, 1982; Amabile, 1983). Of particular interest are those studies analyzing the biological bases of intrinsic motivation and the experiential state associated with it.

Research has been carried out at two levels. The first focuses on the adaptive advantages brought by the motivational process. Here one might include authors using sociobiological approaches (Wilson, 1975; Lumsden and Wilson, 1981) and studies conducted in the field of evolutionary psychology (Barkow, Cosmides and Tooby, 1992). Among the latter, we shall mention Weisfeld (1993), who emphasizes the adaptive value of internal positive states and their expression, with particular attention to their biological basis. The second level focuses more specifically on the relationship between internal motivation, self-determined selective attention, and the functioning of the central nervous system. Here we shall mention the works of Hamilton (1981) and of Hamilton, Haier and Buchsbaum (1984). The latter, for instance, studied the relationship between intrinsic motivation, emotional states, quality of selective attention processes, locus of control, development of the Ego (all functions measured with psychometric instruments), and the electric activity of the central nervous system. These authors claim that intrinsic motivational processes are associated with a positive affective state, high levels of cognitive arousal, elevated development of the Ego, perceived internal locus of control, little tendency to boredom, and also, from a physiological point of view, with electroencephalographic indexes indicating the activation of attention and an increase in cortical activity.

2.3.3 Self-Determination Theory

All of the previously mentioned research lead Deci and Ryan (1985) to formalize more adequately the concept of intrinsic motivation and to integrate it within the wider context of "self-determination theory" (Ryan, Connell and Deci, 1985). This theory (the significance of which for the development of behavior will be further discussed in the following section) is focused on overcoming the sharp opposition between intrinsic and extrinsic motivation. This is achieved by giving the concept of self-determination a central and fundamental role. Although the initial studies pointed out the negative effect of external reinforcement on intrinsic motivation (caused by a shift from an internal to an external locus of causality), later research began to provide contradictory data. Under given circumstances, external rewards were found to increase intrinsic motivation (Harackiewicz, 1979; Ryan, 1982; Ryan, Mims and Koestner, 1983). Thus, it appears that in addition to internally motivated behavior, which is self-determined by definition, externally motivated behavior can also have degrees of self-determination (Deci and Ryan, 1985). More specifically, externally motivated behavior can be considered self-determined when it tallies with the aims and dynamics of the self; namely, when the locus of causality is perceived as being internal (Deci and Ryan, 1985). In these cases, even though external rewards may be present, an individual will perceive his or her own behavior primarily as the result of self-directed contingencies.

In more general terms, using a terminology mentioned earlier, we can define self-determination as the capacity of an individual to actively select (in function of his or her own identity as it developed over time) information from the external environment. This process yields both an increase in selected information and a complex structuring of the system of personal responses to the demands and stimuli coming from the external world (Rigby, Deci, Patrick and Ryan, 1992).

On the basis of these presuppositions, Deci and Ryan (1985) distinguish four types of extrinsic behavioral regulations, laid along a continuum, from the absence to a significant presence of self-determination.

1. **Pure extrinsic motivation (or external regulation):** This mechanism is the basis for those behaviors imposed by particular external conditions, such as agreed upon rewards and punishments. In this case, the subject is forced to act, and even if a small amount of intentionality can be detected, it is present only to a negligible degree in that it is determined by external contingencies. Therefore, there are no volitional aspects present. Here, we are at the heart of the concept of external reinforcement developed by the behaviorist school.

2. **Introjected extrinsic motivation (or introjected regulation):** This process is the basis for those behaviors conditioned by factors

beyond the control of the individual though still concerning his or her internal sphere. Here we are considering behavioral thrusts or pressures tied to elements, such as a sense of guilt or self-esteem. In these cases, individuals act in a given way not because they desire it, but because they feel it must be done in order to feel like a valuable person. This is an internal regulatory mechanism in which actions are controlled by internal forces, but they are not self-determined. Therefore, there is no active selection and the locus of causality is perceived as partially internal, though still external with respect to deeper parts of the self: the action remains external to an integrated sense of identity (Ryan and Connell, 1989).

3. **Identified extrinsic motivation (or identified regulation):** This type of motivation exists when a behavior is dictated by environmental demands and at the same time it tallies with the referential system of the individual, with his or her identity and personal goals. This happens when subjects identify themselves with the values implicit in a given activity and accept the external regulation as their own. The behavior is still instrumental (of an extrinsic nature) but connected with the self. As an example, one may think of students who are highly involved in academic studies, not because of fear of being punished by the family (as in the case of pure extrinsic motivation), nor in order to feel accepted and to feel good about themselves (introjected extrinsic motivation), but because studying is a self-selected goal, since it will lead to a diploma and to the practice of an actively chosen profession corresponding to the characteristics and goals of the self.

4. **Integrated extrinsic motivation (or integrated regulation):** This is the most autonomous or self-determined form of extrinsic motivation, and it results from the integration (or reciprocal assimilation) of separate identifications in a cohesive sense of self. This process is characteristic of behaviors still extrinsic, since they are not associated with a subjective experience representing a reward in itself, as in the case of intrinsic motivation. However, these behaviors are highly integrated and tally with the subjectivity of the individual as it was formed through past experiences,

and they allow the development of a personal identity toward an increasingly greater complexity of the self. The integration of the information coming from the external world with the data structured in consciousness is achieved when the individual assimilates this information and avoids disorganized internal states, even in the presence of stimuli potentially in opposition to or incongruent with it.

The continuous elaboration and integration of new information increases the complexity of the cognitive structures and schemata. This is the case since internalized and integrated data will always be of an increasing number and of a greater complexity, thus leading to the development of a flexible identity:

> For example, a parent might identify with being an authority figure as well as being a friend to his or her children. These two roles may be equally valued, and they may seem to conflict, but the roles can become integrated through a "creative synthesis" . . . the two values could co-exist harmoniously with each other and with other aspects of the self, thus not causing psychological stress for the individual (Rigby, Deci, Patrick and Ryan, 1992, p. 170).

This last type of regulation therefore represents the most autonomous form of extrinsic motivation. The individual feels that the environmental forces are not threatening coercions, but rather, offer relevant information in order for the individual to make meaningful choices.

This is a certain kind of psychic functioning that, with intrinsic motivation, represents the presupposition of an integrated development of the self. The individual experiences choices as intentional, thinks there is autonomous growth, and is able to integrate the data coming from the external reality with the data present in consciousness. Consequently, even insignificant, banal, or conflictual daily activities can give rise to an integrated moment and to the development of the self. At the same time, psychic processes characteristic of intrinsic motivation are also present, such as cognitive flexibility, depth of information processing, and creativity.

56

Integrated extrinsic motivation differs from intrinsic motivation in that, as we noted, only behavior coming from the latter constitutes an experiential reward. The operationalization and the lived experience associated with these behaviors is the ultimate reason for their coming into being. Integrated extrinsic motivation, on the other hand, is still the basis for instrumental behavior but shares with intrinsic motivation the profound feeling of autonomy and self-determination.

The analysis carried out by Deci and Ryan (1985) concerning the typology of extrinsic motivation (which is derived from a series of precise experimental studies), introduces an important novelty, while at the same time avoiding a sharp separation between intrinsic and extrinsic motivation.

These authors, however, do not take the motivational aspect to be as fundamental as the more general aspects of integration and internalization. In this way, they locate themselves within the domain of emergent theories of behavior. The starting point of their work is the consideration that human beings innately tend to an increase in cognitive, affective, and behavioral complexity. This claim, based, as we said, on specific data (cf. Condry and Stokker, 1992), derives its theoretical presuppositions from the concepts of hierarchical integration (Werner, 1948), organization (Piaget, 1954), development (Rogers, 1963), and enlargement of the self (Angyal, 1965). Deci and Ryan summarize their thought in the concept of organic integration: a natural process, based on the possibility of self-determination, which operates simultaneously at the intra-individual level (where it allows for greater organization and integration of the personality) and at the inter-individual level (where it leads to more adaptive and satisfactory relations as regards social interaction). The tendency toward integration takes into account that the development of behavior may take place not only when the individuals direct psychic energy and actions toward goals and social objectives congruent with their own most personal motivations (that is following their own intrinsic motivation). The complexity of both social behavior and its development also takes place through this process of internalization and integration of values, rules, and elements of the external world in general. The latter may not motivate or interest the individual in an immediate way, but they allow a feeling of autonomy and at the same time connection with other members of the social groups to which one belongs.

This allows us to analyze in greater depth the relationship between motivation, development of personality, and external context. The internalization and integration of external behavioral instructions allow the individual both to develop an identity springing from internally motivated experience and to grow through the integration of behavioral instructions that ground instrumental behavior. In other words, individuals assimilate and internalize data associated with activities which, on the one hand, allow them to feel capable of choosing freely and hence of self-determination, and, on the other hand, allow them to feel integrated with the surrounding society and to be recognized in their own social role. Extrinsic motivation is therefore no longer seen as an unavoidable and forced element imposed on the free psychological selection of the individual, because the latter is present insofar as behavior guided by external rewards is assimilated and perceived by the individual as not contradicting previously established goals.

Thus we have (1) the tendency to develop new information at the cognitive and behavioral levels; (2) the compatibility of this new information with the information already present in the individual; and (3) the connection between the development of personality and social rules. This model describes a complex behavioral system that goes beyond the domain of studies concerning motivational systems, and it establishes itself within the domain of general theories dealing with personality formation and the development of individual and social behavior.

In the past few years, there have been new contributions to the domain of intrinsic motivation. Several studies have investigated the idea of optimal learning in relation to the autonomous development of the personality. The primary areas of investigation have been education (Ryan, Connell and Plant, 1990; Lepper and Cordova, 1992; Heyman and Dweck, 1992; Boggiano et al., 1992), family (Grolnick and Ryan, 1989; Ryan and Stiller, 1991), and work (Deci, Connell and Ryan, 1989).

Recent literature points out some basic issues relevant to our discussion. The Rochester school continued to study the relation between intrinsic motivation, extrinsic motivation, self-determination, and development of behavior (Deci and Ryan, 1991), reiterating the presence of an innate thrust to explore, understand, and integrate oneself with the environment. This thrust is present from birth and does not need external forces to come into being. This innate motivation is the basis for the acquisition of cognitive, affective, and relational capacities, and for the processes involved in the formation of the personality. The evolution of the self, learning, and cognitive development are facilitated by social contexts allowing for and stimulating (1) autonomy, (2) a space for individual capacities to express themselves, and (3) relational interaction (Deci and Ryan, 1991; Rigby, Deci, Patrick and Ryan, 1992).

Other research groups hold slightly different positions. The work of Harter and Jackson (1992) is of particular interest. These authors, although beginning from a different point of view, also oppose the sharp dichotomy between extrinsic and intrinsic motivation. On the basis of their data and observing that the motivational orientation of their subjects follows a normal distribution, Harter and Jackson point out that the traditional dichotomy between the two types of motivation, based on the concept of motivation as a stable trait of personality, is no longer valid. Motivation seems to be a process related to the capacity of individuals to behave differently in different contexts using flexible motivational strategies.

Boggiano and colleagues are of the same opinion (1992). According to them, motivational orientations are situation-specific. This flexibility fosters the perception and execution of autonomous behavioral strategies, which, in turn, allow for the full development of an individual as understood by the Rochester school. The theoretical orientation of this last group, founded by E. L. Deci (who also defined the concept of intrinsic motivation), seems to be among the most advanced. Its soundness is reflected by the fact that their contributions meet the requirements of a modern psychological theory (requirements analyzed in the first chapter and summarized at the beginning of the second), which we will now review.

2.3.4 Contribution to an Evolving and Organized View of Behavior

Our initial hypothesis suggested the existence of a teleonomic project within psychic processes. We have pointed out, in general terms, the two elements that should be included in such a project:

1. the replication in time of a given psychic organization and its contents;
2. the tendency of the replicative psychic organization to increase the complexity of its information.

We have looked for psychological theories that focus, more or less explicitly, on such teleonomies. The concept of self-determination (proposed by Deci and Ryan) in this respect seems to be of particular interest.

It has been repeatedly pointed out that intrinsic motivational processes are characterized, according to various authors, by a feeling of autonomy, free will, and self-determination. Individuals perceive an action as derived from their own internal strengths (internal locus of causality), and not as derived from environmental stimuli to which they respond mechanically. Furthermore, the possibility of self-determination is strictly related to the active selection of data from external contexts. The feeling of curiosity and discovery are accompanied by the perception of being able to approach the data derived from the external world and by being able to approach real situations in an autonomous and innovative way. All these elements seem to fully satisfy an emergent and negentropic view of behavior. Nevertheless, intrinsic motivation alone, as opposed to extrinsic motivation, does not meet our second theoretical requirement, namely, the replication of psychic organization and contents. In other words, intrinsic motivation in itself can also be satisfied in single, and at times sporadic, external situations. The latter allow for the feeling of actively managing attention and action, but at the same time they are not part of a larger and more general path of development and therefore are not associated with the replication of ordered regularities.

In order to satisfy this second aspect of teleonomy, it is also not sufficient to take into consideration the other element of intrinsic motivation, namely, competence. If it is true that in order to feel capable of facing environmental demands it is necessary to have lived through experiences that, being related to the environment, lead to the development of personal capacities, we also have to keep in mind that intrinsic motivation generally tends to represent an optimal phenomenological event in momentary relation to the environment. Therefore, if intrinsic motivation is considered independently from the overall course of life, rich in environmental demands stimulating extrinsic motivation, it cannot offer a paradigm of general interest. It can only explain single given moments of our relationship with the external world, which cannot be considered as central to the formation of the self.

If, on the other hand, we shift our attention (following Deci and Ryan) to the concept of self-determination, it is then possible to enlarge this paradigm by taking into account the process of the formation of the self in relation to extrinsic motivation and environmental demands.

When individuals in situations of integrated extrinsic motivation aim their own behavior at instrumental external goals and integrate the latter with their own general life objectives, they reproduce the information already present in their internal world and in their own affective, cognitive, and behavioral schemata; it is this information that forms their personal identity. At the same time, they behave in a self-determined way. In this case, the autonomy can be seen in the choice of integrating parts of the external world exerting an active pressure on the individual (such as extrinsic behavioral stimuli), which are accepted because they are in harmony with his or her identity.

Self-determination understood in connection with extrinsic motivation will then find a fuller and clearer manifestation in internally motivated behaviors. Overall, the theory of self-determination points out the possibility of an integrated formation of the self in harmony with the external world. Intrinsic and extrinsic motivational processes in their most self-determined forms allow for a continuous, mutually determining relationship between the social world (which offers stimuli and rules) and the individual world (which adapts itself to external demands, integrating them with the individual's own past experiences, and also actively discovers the surrounding reality and creates new self-determined information). In short, we have a mechanism that relates the formation of the self to the social world. The stable personality trait characterizing an integrated regulation and development does not correspond, from this point of view, to the motivational orientation (either intrinsic or extrinsic), but rather to the capacity for using the two kinds of motivation in a flexible way with the aim of achieving self-determination.

Thus, once again, the individual achieves both of the essential elements of psychic teleonomy: repetition and evolution of information. This comes about not only through the expression of personality components (as formed by past experiences) and through the replication of social rules and demands that are acted upon and internalized, but also through free and unforeseen selections of environmental data activated by internally motivated behaviors not mechanically conditioned by the external world.

The data gathered by the authors mentioned in this section seem to demonstrate that this harmonious integration of continuity and development and of personal and social regulation, represents a behavioral mechanism common to all individuals. Regarding this issue, we shall report two examples of psychosocial functioning derived from non-Western cultures that point out the characteristics and the centrality of this mechanism as it manifests itself in sociocultural organization.

The native societies of North America, especially those of Sino-Mongolian origin, show a complex and refined apparatus of psychological and social regulation, which has been analyzed by several anthropological (Reichard, 1950) and psychological studies (Massimini, Csikszentmihalyi and Delle Fave, 1988; Inghilleri, 1993b; Inghilleri and Delle Fave, 1996).

The Navajo culture has a vision of the world in which all elements (physical, biological, psychic, and spiritual) are harmoniously organized in a mutually interconnected way. Yet this balance is maintained and transmitted over time only by virtue of continuous changes and imbalances. Novelties, extraneous elements, and the unforeseen, are therefore permitted and even sought after. This society has a remarkable means of reestablishing order and of integrating the unknown in what is known – mainly through powerful ceremonies that are deeply significant to each individual involved. These numerous ceremonies, rituals, and chants allow for a specific "cure" – that is, the resolution of conflicts and personal or social disturbances. Individuals are then able to feel in harmony with their own identities and with the social organization. The individual is understood as introducing novelties within the existing social rules. These novelties are brought about by intrinsic motivation and their connected processes (Inghilleri, 1993b; Inghilleri and Delle Fave, 1996). The social rules and organization are capable of assimilating and re-elaborating in an integrated way such innovations. This is done by sustaining a sense of the individual's autonomy in relation to the often-rigid norms of the tribe, which represent the extrinsic elements. In this way, the culture can be both transmitted over time and transformed in function of historical changes. This psychosocial structure allowed for the survival, for instance, of the Navajo society at times of massive cultural transformation, which followed upon contact with the Anglo society.

Another case in which regularity and innovation are integrated into the same cultural context is given by situations of rapid governmental change in third-world nations, at times brought about by revolution. We are referring to countries in which the colonial government has more or less completely destroyed the native cultural tradition. The achievement of independence offers the possibility of rediscovering these roots and traditions, but in the majority of cases the original cultural identity has vanished. These nations (demonstrating the tendency to reconstruct a society around an original replicative nucleus) tend to look for symbols in their recent history that embody the values of their past by translating them into current terms related to current values. This tendency also seems to demonstrate, on the social side, the fundamental necessity of integrating regularities (the traditional nucleus) and changes (political independence or revolution).

This is what happened in Nicaragua after the 1979 revolution. The new government, in order to reestablish a national spirit, did not resort to ancient Indian historical figures, which had been largely forgotten. Instead, the government symbolized the historical change by connecting it with the traditional figure of a non-commissioned officer named Sandino (who in the 1920s proudly stood against the foreign domination), thereby awakening the independent spirit of the country. Hence the name "Sandinista" was given to the Nicaraguan government in the 1980s.

In a country where the great majority of the population was in their teens, a symbol such as Sandino well-represented the synthesis of historical tradition and change. In taking this path, the government of the time was therefore seeking to bring about an economic and social development where individual property and values could be integrated with social ones, and at the same time where rural tradition and modernization (largely brought about by international organizations) could be harmoniously connected. In accordance with this plan, the population was sustained in its daily family life, in school, and in work and recreational settings, thus attempting to integrate rules and tradition with change and individual freedom. This interaction manifested itself not only in ideological terms, but in the actual daily relations between intrinsic and extrinsic motivation (Inghilleri, 1986; Terranova-Cecchini and Panzeri, 1986; Rushdie, 1987).

This is not the place to analyze the partial failure of this sociopolitical initiative, but we may say that one of its main problems, at least at the symbolic level, was that Nicaragua found itself poised between two opposing political poles (liberalism, encouraged by the United States and bureaucratic Marxism–Leninism, sustained, at the time, by the Soviet Union), which in that place and time did not allow for the accomplishment of a project that implied, at both the social and individual levels, the integration of self-determination and originality with tradition and continuity.

2.4 OPTIMAL EXPERIENCE

2.4.1 Theoretical Roots

The second general theory to be discussed here, on the basis of the theoretical necessities exposed in the introductory sections, is the theory of *flow*, or optimal experience, elaborated at The University of Chicago (Csikszentmihalyi, 1975). Before considering the specifics of this theory, we shall briefly analyze the cultural matrix from which it emerged.

A first point of reference is certainly the debate regarding the relationship between intrinsic and extrinsic motivation and the centrality of the concept of self-determination. Second, it is useful to keep in mind, even if only as an indirect theoretical framework, the role of "humanistic" psychology, grounded in the works of Abraham Maslow and Carl Rogers. Maslow (1954, 1968) points out the self-realization factor as a privileged moment in the development of identity. The latter is enriched by "peak experiences," very intense and involving events during which the subject perceives the object as a whole. This perception is disinterested, meaning that it is disconnected from considerations regarding the utility of the object or from any particular aim. The object is perceived as unique, and it occupies the entire space of consciousness; thus, it transcends the opposition between form and content (Maslow, 1959). Rogers also focuses on the value of those single experiences by means of which individuals perceive the meaning of their identities and are able to develop their behaviors (Rogers, 1961).

A third and more important point of reference is the group of theories concerned with the problem of disorder, or conflict, within the psychic system (Csikszentmihalyi, 1988b). In this area, we find, for instance, studies concerned with basic negative emotions (Ekman, 1972; Izard, 1977; Izard, Kagan and Zajonc, 1984); studies in clinical psychology and psychiatry concerned with the alterations of affective states, in particular, depression (Davison and Neale, 1986); and studies in cognitive social psychology, in particular, the theory of cognitive dissonance (Festinger, 1957), which points out the necessity of resolving cognitive conflicts when faced with discordant information. In the latter case, using familiar terminology, we are faced with psychic entropy. This entropy occurs when the stimuli selected from the external world do not match the information present in consciousness; or at a more phenomenological level, when certain internal states are perceived as contradicting the individual's goals. Thus, a negative experience emerges (characterized by feelings of anxiety, boredom, and confusion) to different degrees according to the structure of identity and the type of information processed (Csikszentmihalyi, 1988b).

2.4.2 Emergent Motivation

Csikszentmihalyi's theory begins with a general analysis of motivations and their classification. By motivation we mean the focusing of psychic energy (in its cognitive and emotional aspects) on given goals (Csikszentmihalyi, 1982, 1985).

The proposed classification derives from (1) an extended review, carried out by Csikszentmihalyi, of the existent literature (Csikszentmihalyi, 1985); (2) a theoretical discussion of the above-mentioned relationship between consciousness and attention; and (3) numerous studies on the quality of experience and motivational characteristics, found in different contexts, carried out by The University of Chicago research group (Csikszentmihalyi, Larson and Prescott, 1977; Csikszentmihalyi and Larson, 1978, 1984; Csikszentmihalyi and Graef, 1980; Csikszentmihalyi and Kubey, 1981; Csikszentmihalyi, 1981; Csikszentmihalyi and Figurski, 1982).

An initial distinction is made between exogenous motivations, which are perceived by the subject as imposed by the external environment, and endogenous motivations, which are perceived by the subject as originating from his or her own internal world (Kruglansky, 1975; Csikszentmihalyi, 1978b). These latter are the most important ones, because even though our everyday behavior is largely regulated by external forces, these are accepted only in so far as they are in harmony with personal motivations (Csikszentmihalyi, 1985). This has been also pointed out by the previously mentioned studies on self-determination.

Csikszentmihalyi (1985) proposes a classification that aims to include all endogenous motivations operating in everyday behavior, while avoiding simplification and the reductionistic explanation of observations. Such simplifications can easily emerge, according to Csikszentmihalyi, from methodological necessities characteristic of laboratory research.

This classification (Fig. 2.1) is based on two dichotomies: the distinction between individual and social processes and goals; and the distinction between open and closed systems, that is, according to whether the motivations lead to closed or open explanations. In other words, according to whether the motivations depend on already "given" informational systems – for instance, the instructions contained in the genetic or cultural codes, or to whether they emerge in an original way as a result of experience, in a way that they cannot be traced back to preexisting determining factors.

It should be noted that such a classification avoids, and in a certain sense overcomes, the often-cited distinction between biological and learned motivations. According to Csikszentmihalyi, every motivation has a biological cause or substrate, and is at the same time shaped by learned factors. Therefore, we are not reiterating a sterile debate regarding the dichotomy of nature versus nurture. Rather, we are interested in verifying whether a behavior can be explained on the basis of causes already present in the organism or in the environment (closed situation), or whether it is derived in an original way from the specific interaction of an organism with the external context (open situation).

This plasticity of motivation had already been pointed out by Gordon Allport with his concept of "functional autonomy" (Allport, 1961). Figure 2.1 therefore represents a two-by-two table whose cells include different types of motivation.

67

	Primarily Intra-Individual Processes	Primarily Inter-Individual Processes
Primarily Closed Systemic Goals	1. "Needs" Hunger Thirst Safety Optimal Acivation, etc.	2. "Socialization" Sex Affiliation Achievement Presented life theme
Primarily Open Systemic Goals	4. "Emergent Motives" Intrinsic motivation Flow Self-development Discovered life theme	3. "Cultivation" Values Social Goals Identification Ideologies, etc.

Figure 2.1. A simple typology of endogenous motives. (Csikszentmihalyi, 1985, p.96)

1. **Individual processes – closed systems.** This area contains the motivations concerning intra-individual processes and goals. These are closed systems in that they are bound by biological or internal systems of information aimed at satisfying homeostatic needs. These are the types of motivation originally taken into consideration by the authors of the behaviorist school, starting with Hull (1943). These types of motivation are at the origin of behaviors associated with hunger, thirst, or security needs.

2. **Social processes – closed systems.** The motivations included in this cell are still connected with the properties of closed systems, but they concern inter-individual processes and goals, or the processes and goals concerned with the relationship between the individual and the culture. Individuals perceive their own actions as guided by internal forces, but in

fact these derive from external forces acting through social-ization and educational processes. A person partially builds the themes of his or her own life on the basis of stimuli or models introduced by external contexts or other people (Bandura, 1977).

3. **Social processes – open systems.** This type of motivation derives from the interaction of the individual with the culture, its symbols and rules. In this interaction the person not only internalizes behavioral instructions, but also elaborates, trans-forms, and adapts them to internal needs. Individuals more or less significantly change the symbolic or rule systems with which they are confronted. They will address part of their psy-chic energy toward new social goals or symbols. In other words, individuals tend to reinterpret in a new way scientific, religious, moral, and political ideas, and tend to behave accord-ing to such modifications (Csikszentmihalyi and Rochberg-Halton, 1981). If the personal reorganizations of these goals are then spread throughout the culture and become part of its moti-vational structure, they will represent a close system for the fol-lowing generations. In other words, if a cultural innovation produced by the members of a minority group is then spread to the entire population, it will, in turn, be at the origin of closed motivations, belonging to the previously described cell.

4. **Individual processes – open systems.** This cell includes those motivations (concerning individual processes and goals) discovered by a person in an unforeseen way during his or her interaction with the environment. These motivations, within an individual's life span, play the same role that a new value emerging within a society plays in the history of the culture.

We can define these motivations as emergent in that they do not preexist nor do they find their origin in genes (biological instruc-tions) or in learned behavioral schemata (internalized cultural instructions). These motivations derive from the interaction with the environment, colored by the specific quality of an unprece-dented subjective experience (Csikszentmihalyi, 1985).

2.4.3 The Study of Subjective Experience

The basic idea behind The University of Chicago research group and its theoretical perspective is the centrality of subjective experience, and the importance of the thorough study of this experience at the very moment in which it occurs in real-life contexts. In fact, it seems that contemporary psychology increasingly points to the phenomenology of experience as a way to achieve a real understanding of behavior.

Even within the psychoanalytic domain – where sometimes distant causal mechanisms were given a privileged position in the understanding of current behaviors – one can find a new interest in the role played by the quality of psychic processes at the time of their emergence, independent of their deeper roots. We are not simply referring to the renewed interest in Ego-psychology (Hartmann, 1958), but also to recent psychoanalytic discussions concerning the possible primacy, within psychic dynamics, of the quality of secondary processes (Severi, 1992). We can interpret Severi's thought as a suggestion, within the anthropological debate between diffusionists and structuralists, that both positions agree on attributing a primary role to the subject's experience. According to the first approach, the subject's experience is at the basis of historical behaviors; according to the second, it is at the basis of the work of fundamental structures. The universality of the concept, therefore, does not reside in primary representations, but in the modification of relational systems: which is to say, not in primitive psychic materials, but in the process of transformation – in connection with subjective experience – of these materials into cultural symbols.

In other words, it seems that there is an increasing interest in studying what an individual feels, experiences, and does when the various mechanisms proposed by psychoanalysis are operating. And this not only within the domain of the therapist–patient relationship, but in the broader sense according to which the quality of experience and secondary cognitions can take on an active role within the dynamics of the psyche.

To return to The University of Chicago research group, according to Csikszentmihalyi:

> Subjective experience exists in consciousness. It consists of thoughts, feelings, sensations – in short, information that effects a discriminable change in awareness. . . . Focusing attention on the interplay of data in consciousness is what we call experience (Csikszentmihalyi, 1982, p.15).

It should be noted that this definition agrees with the definition offered earlier concerning the relationship between consciousness and attention. In particular, Csikszentmihalyi claims:

> Relating information from outside sources to states of consciousness must be an ordered process, and therefore it requires inputs of energy. . . . The more relevant source of energy that keeps consciousness in an ordered state is information. Consciousness becomes disorganized when the input of information is either too complex or too simple. This can be due to either external causes – the environment contains too many or too few stimuli – or to malfunctions of attentional processes that allow excessive or inadequate information to reach consciousness (Csikszentmihalyi, 1982, pp.15–16).

Given the importance of subjective experience, the Chicago school has elaborated specific methods for its study. The methodological objective was to describe variations in the investment of psychic energy occurring in real-life.

This requires an accurate and measurable description of three basic behavioral elements: (1) the external dimension, which is to say peoples' life-contexts, (2) the characteristics of peoples' actions, and (3) changes in the subject's thoughts, emotions, and motivations. The aim is therefore to determine possible regularities within the flow of experiences, such as states of increased concentration, of anxiety, of good and bad moods, and the presence of intrinsic motivation, and to correlate these elements with (1) the characteristics of the person (gender, age, occupation, education,

71

marital status, ethnicity, or even type of personality, evaluated by adequate instruments), (2) the characteristics of the situation (type of activity, location, and time), and (3) the characteristics of the social context (solitude or type of company).

In order to achieve this aim, Csikszentmihalyi and his group elaborated a particular method called the Experience Sampling Method (ESM), or method for the study of daily experience (Csikszentmihalyi, Larson and Prescott, 1977; Larson and Csikszentmihalyi, 1983). This procedure consists of giving subjects a simple wristwatch or beeper programmed to give an acoustic or vibratory signal at random intervals. Subjects are also given a booklet containing short, identical questionnaires. When the acoustic or vibratory signal is given, the subject is expected to fill out one of the questionnaires. Subjects therefore describe several times a day (about eight signals a day are given) and for several days (usually a week, in addition to a pilot day) their own experiential state as it develops in different external contexts.

The standard version of the ESM provides a series of questions concerning the specific time, location, company, main activity, secondary activities, and thought content. All these questions require open-ended answers, which therefore need appropriate codes for analysis and categorization. There are also numerical scales measuring levels of motivation, concentration, competence, and of perceived environmental demands. There are also categorical scales measuring levels of affect, activity, and cognitive efficiency.

This method provides a self-description of internal states that can then be correlated with the characteristic of the external environment and with the subject's behavior. The ultimate aim is an accurate and objective description of subjective states in real-life, while respecting the parameters given by the so-called "naturalistic" studies (Denzin and Lincoln, 1994).

The type of questions asked can obviously vary accordingly to the type of research conducted and according to the theoretical constructs taken as starting points, but the data gathered in real-life have to remain analyzable. The ESM has been in fact demonstrated to have good reliability and validity (Csikszentmihalyi, 1986; Csikszentmihalyi and Larson, 1987).

This method is accompanied by other procedures, which also aim at the analysis of subjective experience concerning daily behaviors. These other data are gathered in a traditional way, with paper-and-pencil questionnaires, reconstructing past experiences at a somewhat later time (Csikszentmihalyi and Csikszentmihalyi Selega, 1988).

2.4.4 Characteristics of Flow

Starting from the theoretical postulates described in the previous sections and, most of all, on the basis of the numerous data gathered, Csikszentmihalyi and his colleagues develop a particular theory concerning the quality of experience, the development of behavior, and the formation of personality, paying particular attention to cultural evolution. We are referring to the theory of flow or optimal experience (Csikszentmihalyi, 1975, 1990, 1993; Csikszentmihalyi and Massimini, 1985; Csikszentmihalyi and Csikszentmihalyi Selega, 1988).

The first formulation of the theory derived from a study investigating the reasons for choosing arduous activities, often dangerous and at times risky, in situations lacking material rewards or when such rewards were only a secondary element. Hundreds of subjects were tested: rock-climbers, dancers, chess players, artists, and renowned surgeons. The investigation revealed that these subjects had in common a similar and positive emotional state that led them to repeat the experience over time. This was called *flow experience* in that various subjects used the metaphor of a current transporting them effortlessly in order to describe their experiences (Csikszentmihalyi, 1975).

Since then several studies have confirmed the presence of this type of experience and have pointed out the psychic components shaping it. These studies have also found that this is a quite rare phenomenon; however, it is not specific to certain individuals, activities, or cultures. Studies including young and old people, men and women, students, workers, and retired people, Japanese and Koreans, Thailandese and Native Americans, Italians and Germans, Americans and Indians, show that the experience of flow concerns all of us and can develop in very different contexts (Csikszentmihalyi and Csikszentmihalyi Selega, 1988; Csikszentmihalyi, 1990; Massimini and Inghilleri, 1986). An active research group working at the Psychology Institute at the University of Milan's medical school gathered more than 7,000 interviews on flow in different populations throughout the world, with subjects ranging from 7 to 87 years old, belonging to very different social classes, and working in very different settings. In all cases, the structure of the experience reported by subjects remains the same, although the context in which it emerges or the activity that brings it about varies (Massimini, Csikszentmihalyi and Delle Fave, 1988; Csikszentmihalyi and Rathunde, 1993).

Flow is a complex state in which cognitive, motivational, and affective processes interact in an ordered way, and are integrated with respect to (1) the structure and the demands of the external world as they developed over time and (2) the external context present at the time of the experience. From a phenomenological point of view, flow is, for Csikszentmihalyi, a subjective state according to which an individual is so involved in the moment as to "forget" all other experiential elements (as, for instance, past memories, future projects, tiredness) in order to focus his or her cognition and become immersed in the situation at hand. The experience is characterized by a deep sense of involvement that triggers a sense of well-being and therefore represents an internal reward *per se*. The experience of flow is made possible by a harmonious copresence of a series of elements belonging to the subject's internal world, and of a series of elements present in the external context.

A first condition is the presence of clear and noncontradictory goals, and of an external context and situation providing clear and prompt signals and feedback to the subject's behavior. This is to say that subjects are aware, easily and without cognitive effort, of how events are proceeding and what are the consequences of their actions.

A second condition necessary in order for the experience of flow to occur is the presence of balance between the opportunity for action and the challenges present in the external environment, on the one hand, and the capacities and skills at the subject's disposal (built through past experiences) required to face the environmental demands, on the other. It should be noted that this balance is perceived at the subjective level. In other words, it depends both on the objective competence of an individual and the intensity of the external demands, and on the individual's subjective evaluation of environmental challenges and personal skills.

This balance entails an automatic control over the situation at hand. The subject is completely immersed and involved in what is happening. The concentration is deep. The distinction between actor and action disappears. The individual is extremely aware of the surrounding reality and personal actions, but this awareness arises without cognitive effort and without the subject having to control personal behavior through self-observation. In a certain sense, one "is aware of his actions but not of the awareness itself" (Csikszentmihalyi , 1975, p.38). In this way the entire psychic energy, that is, the attention processes, can focus on the situation at hand without having to be partially directed toward evaluating the behavior.

When all these elements are present in consciousness, the activity tends to become autotelic: The activity itself becomes the very reason for which it is carried out.[1] The feeling of an ordered psychic organization, the balance between challenges and skills, the automatic perception of optimal functioning, are accompanied by a positive affective state, and by a feeling of joy and free choice, which lead the subject to dwell in that situation and to seek it out. Table 2.1 is a summary of the characteristics of the experience of flow according to Csikszentmihalyi.

2.4.5 Balance Between Challenges and Skills

Flow is an experience that comes about only when all the factors found in Table 2.1 are simultaneously present. The interrelation of

Table 2.1 *Characteristic Dimensions of the Flow Experience (partially derived from Csikszentmihalyi, Rathunde, 1993, p.60).*

Clear goals	It is clear what should be done.
Immediate feedback	Precise information is given about how things are going.
Challenges/skills balance	Opportunities for action and external world demands are perceived to be in harmony with the internal skills available to face such demands.
Concentration on the task at hand	Irrelevant stimuli disappear from consciousness: the entire attention is focused on the situation at hand; worries and concerns are temporarily eliminated.
Loss of self-consciousness	The subject does not control, from the outside, his or her own behavior; transcendence of ego boundaries; sense of growth and of being part of some greater entity.
Action and awareness merge	There is a sense of aware, ordered, and reversible "fusion" of self and environment.
Sense of automatic control	The control is said to be automatic because it takes place without cognitive effort and without self-observation.
Altered sense of time	Time seems to pass more slowly or (usually) more quickly than normal.
Presence of intrinsic motivation	The experience becomes autotelic; the subject dwells in the situation because the latter fulfills him or her completely: a sense of intrinsic motivation and self-determination are present.

these factors leads to an optimization of experience. Among the elements present in Table 2.1, the balance between challenges and skills – perceived by the individual at a given moment – is of particular importance. In fact, Csikszentmihalyi claims that

76

optimal experience may be further defined in terms of two dimensions: what there is to do and what one is capable of doing (Csikszentmihalyi, 1982, p.16).

In order for this experience to occur, a main requirement must be met: The individual must have the ability to face the situation; that is, his or her skills must be comparable to the degree of complexity of the challenges at hand.

We must think of the skills not in terms of physical ability or intelligence, but in terms of the amount of information an individual has gathered in order to accomplish a given activity or to face a given situation. Furthermore, the level of balance between challenges and skills depends, as we have seen, on subjective control: Individuals can interpret both environmental demands and their own skills in various ways. Consequently, we have to take into consideration the degree of balance not only at an objective level, but also on the basis of possible subjective distortions. For instance, a highly competent individual can, in certain situations, evaluate him or herself as incapable of facing the situation and consequently not have a positive experience.

The relationship between challenges and skills can yield different combinations, summarized in Figure 2.2. The latter points out graphically the relationship between challenges (vertical axes) and skills (horizontal axes).

If one perceives environmental demands as too challenging and difficult with respect to one's skills, one will experience anxiety (Csikszentmihalyi, 1975). Therefore, if the task requires the analysis of an elevated amount of information or of overly complex information, the subject feels inadequate and a complete involvement in the situation is difficult. A part of the subject's attention processes are directed toward self-observation; thus, the cognitive focus is lost and the level of affectivity is lowered.

The opposite is true when the environmental demands are too simple or when they are perceived as such: They do not require the complete investment of psychic energy. The action, in these cases, is neither demanding nor stimulating. Again, the attention processes are disturbed, the subject lacks concentration, and the

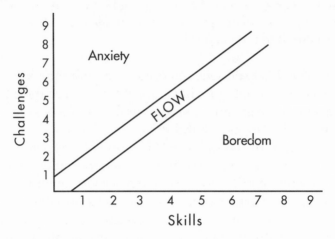

Figure 2.2. The relationship between challenges and skills: flow, anxiety, and boredom. (Csikszentmihalyi and Csikszentmihalyi Selega, 1988, p.259)

affective state is altered. The emerging condition is one of boredom, and consequently, there is no positive experience.

2.4.6 Why Is the Flow Experience Optimal?

At this point it might be useful to ask why people live the experience of flow as optimal and why they seek it out. Different explanations can be derived from different psychological theories. One explanation might hold that seeking a flow experience is the result of trying to satisfy repressed wishes, as, for instance, the ones deriving from Oedipal aggressiveness. According to psychoanalysis, individuals tend to repeat situations and activities that allow for a mediated resolution of internal instinctual tensions. Another hypothesis offered by a different theoretical perspective might explain flow by means of particular personality traits supposed to lead individuals to seek out stimulation (Zuckerman, 1979).

Both interpretations, which we are employing here only as examples, appeal to deep motivations inherent in the personality, to fixed causal mechanisms, or to causes called by Csikszentmihalyi *distal*. In order to satisfy a given theoretical model, they seem to ignore the common subjective state inherent in all activities of this kind, and they seem to ignore that these activities are intrinsically motivating (Csikszentmihalyi and Rathunde, 1993). In contrast, flow is suggested as a *proximal* cause. The experience occurs not because it satisfies preexisting needs (such as the resolution of a conflict), but because its phenomenology is satisfying *per se.*

Studies regarding flow lead us to consider it as a positive state associated with an experience that is lived as optimal, not because it has already been programmed in our central nervous system to be so, but because a particular organization of consciousness is discovered by interacting with the environment. Furthermore, the experience is not randomly constructed. It depends, as we have seen, on past experiences – that is, on the development of adequate skills derived from continuous interaction with the surrounding environment. These environmental challenges derive from specific cultural contexts, with which we interact for long periods of time, and that share, to different degrees, values, norms, and customs of the society in which we were brought up.

The specificity of this experiential state consists in the rare configuration of an ordered, complex, and integrated organization of psychic functions. Cognitive processes are highly active, the affective state is positive, accompanied by a sense of well-being and involvement, and the highest level of internal motivation (as understood by Deci and Ryan) is present. There is therefore no conflict between the different parts of the psychic system; the internal world adequately responds to the demands of the environment; the entire available psychic energy is invested in the action; and the subject experiences a sense of self-determination and competence. It is this integrated system of interactions that makes the experience optimal. It is the very phenomenology of the experience that allows for it to take place and to be prolonged. Therefore, flow does not mechanically derive from past experiences and dynamics, although it is related to them. Flow depends on the unique configuration of psychic organization, by means of which internal and external demands are joined to create the conditions for a new behavioral and psychic development. In this case conscious processes proceed in an ordered way [. . . and] optimal experience is simply experience that flows according to its own requirements (Csikszentmihalyi, 1982, p.21).

This approach is primarily interested in the formal aspects of subjective experience, not in its contents. This involves a mosaic of experiential components that creates an integrated system of interaction with the environment. Such optimal integration – in particular as far as the balance between challenges and skills is concerned – is the keystone necessary to understand the importance of this experiential state for the development of behavior.

Compare this model with the most recent research regarding biological bases of behavior, in particular, with evolutionary psychology (Barkow, 1991; Barkow, Cosmides and Tooby, 1992). According to the latter, the basic psychological mechanisms are developed for adaptation to the environment. Systems of representation and self-representation, the cognitive map of the environment, cognitive schemata in general, and systems of categorization, are seen as the result of the need for survival in a given and increasingly complex social environment, such as the one present in the first human groups. Consequently, it can be hypothesized that the full immersion in activities with a high degree of challenge, met by adequate skills, could have been a behavioral mechanism quite useful for adaptation.

It is plausible to think that those individuals who have experienced a positive state of consciousness associated with the utilization of their skills in facing onerous environmental demands, found themselves at an advantage as far as survival was concerned. In fact, they might have developed behavioral strategies suitable to their own resources and, at the same time, conducive to exploring new environments in controlled situations. Furthermore, the capacity to face environmental demands and the simultaneous state of internal well-being could have been favorable, as far as cognitive capacities are concerned, to developing a sense of self-esteem and to encouraging respect from others. These two elements, self-esteem and being respected by the other members of a group, could have led, according to the evolutionary view, to adaptive and, in particular, to reproductive advantages in that they might have allowed the acquisition of a high status within the community. In a context in which social functions (such as group hunting) were increasingly important for survival, the fact of holding a high social status, not only on the basis of biological strength, but primarily on the basis of cognitive skills, could have allowed better access to the resources of the group, the acquisition of a stable sexual partner, and the transmission of one's genetic patrimony through offsprings.

The integration of internal well-being, environmental demands, and positive evaluation from other members of the group, seems to offer a basis for understanding the biological roots of this state of consciousness. In fact, the latter allows not only for the achievement of an internal regulation, but also for the development of additional social skills and for the exploration of new environmental paths. It is on the concept of development itself that our discussion will now focus.

2.4.7 Dynamics of Flow

The state of flow is not a static one. Flow implies an increase in complexity in both the internal and external world. The balance of challenges and skills between individuals and their activities is unstable, as Figure 2.3 shows. In Csikszentmihalyi's classical version (1975, 1982, 1985), it is claimed that the point of balance (A_1 in Figure 2.3) leads to a gradual recognition and full experience of one's own skills. Becoming familiar with one's own competence and its application gradually generates the evaluation of one's own skills as being superior to the challenges offered by the environment. Consequently, a situation of imbalance will develop (B_1).

Psychic energy will focus partially on such discrepancies, and the integrated state of flow will be interrupted. However, the subject in this situation will be able to discover new challenges (C_1) and his or her interaction with these will allow for the reemergence of optimal experience (A_2). Such an experiential state, although identical (from a formal point of view and as far as the phenomenology of psychic functioning is concerned) to the

81

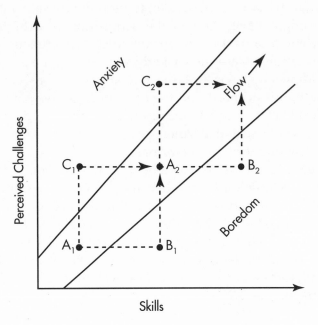

Figure 2.3. The dynamics of flow (Csikszentmihalyi and Rathunde, 1993, p.75).

previous one, involves higher levels of challenges and skills, both of which will be more complex: a development occurs of both internal skills and the situation in which the action takes places, as the latter will be sought after and used to achieve optimal experience.

A better understanding of the dynamic aspects of flow is made possible by a model elaborated in the second half of the 1980s (Carli, 1986; Massimini, Csikszentmihalyi and Carli, 1987). This model evaluates the state of flow starting from the average conditions of an individual's daily life. Each individual develops a specific type of relationship between his or her skills and the environmental demands in different contexts. Some of us tend, on average, to perceive external situations as overly demanding, others tend to perceive them as overly boring, while others will frequently find a balanced relationship. In order to understand the dynamics of subjective states, we must start from this subjective

82

mean. Each activity, during an individual's life span, will present a relationship between challenges and skills that will vary with respect to this mean. The kind and intensity of this variation are the factors leading to positive or negative internal states. The relationship between challenges and skills can therefore be described by means of a circular model divided in eight slices or "channels" (Figure 2.4).

The graph is constituted by Cartesian axes, having on the ordinal the level of challenges and on the abscissa the level of skills. The intersection of the two axes corresponds to the subjective mean of challenges and skills. Each channel represents a particular configuration of the relationship between challenges and skills with respect to an individual's mean. A specific experiential state is associated with this relationship, meaning a certain organization of consciousness as far as cognitive, affective, and motivational functions are concerned; that is, as they are taken into consideration by the theory of flow.[2] We shall now proceed to describe the different situations expressed by these channels as they emerge from the analysis of research data (Carli, 1986; Csikszentmihalyi and Rathunde, 1993).

- **Channel 1,** *arousal,* includes those situations in which the skills are within the mean range while the challenges are above the individual's mean. A subjective state of arousal is present, accompanied by high concentration and relatively positive affective states.

- **Channel 2,** *flow,* corresponds to the classic state of flow. Perceived challenges and skills are in balance and at a level above the individual's mean. All the variables associated with flow are present and have values above the mean: the subject is internally motivated and concentrated; the affective state is extremely positive; and the perceived control of the situation is also elevated. It should also be noticed, however, that in some analyses, the experiential state of channel 2 is very similar, as far as its organization is concerned, to that of channel 1 (Csikszentmihalyi and Nakamura, 1989; Delle Fave and Massimini, 1992).

83

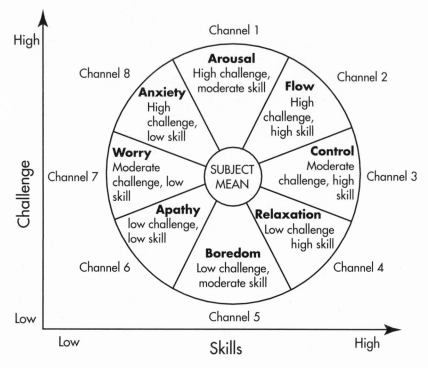

Figure 2.4. A model for the analysis of experience. Perceived challenge is on the ordinate, perceived skill is on the abscissa (Csikszentmihalyi and Rathunde, 1993, p.69, modified according to Figure 1, p.31 in Csikszentmihalyi, 1997).

- **Channel 3,** *control,* indicates high skills meeting moderate challenges, but still close to the subjective mean. The corresponding experiential state is high on positive affect, but lower on concentration and activity.

- **Channel 4,** *relaxation,* was originally identified with the state of boredom as a function of high skills and low challenges (i.e., below the mean). However, empirical results have suggested that in such situations subjects report generally positive affect, and the overall phenomenological state resembles relaxation more than boredom (Csikszentmihalyi, 1997).

84

- **Channel 5,** *boredom,* is defined by moderate skills and low challenges. This is a situation that is definitely negative, lacking in affective, cognitive, and motivational arousal, and that corresponds to the usual definition of boredom.

- **Channel 6,** *apathy,* is particularly interesting. In this case, skills and challenges are balanced (as in cases generally defined as optimal by the classical model), but this balance is located at a level lower than the subjective mean. The experiential state is generally very negative, accompanied by extremely low levels of motivation and cognitive efficiency and by negative feelings regarding oneself and others. The subject is disengaged from the environment. Consciousness is not focused around a goal that might allow for behavioral development.

- **Channel 7,** *worry,* indicates skills lower than the mean and moderate challenges. It is an intermediate experiential state low on affect but moderate on activation, which tends to the state of anxiety, typical of the following channel.

- **Channel 8,** *anxiety,* represents situations in which the challenges are high and the skills are low (a situation similar to the one already encountered in the classical model, as far as the type of imbalance is concerned). The experiential situation is negative: concentration and motivational arousal are present, but they are accompanied by difficulty of concentration and negative affects.

The map of the different experiential states proposed by this model is useful in that it points out the dynamic aspects of flow and its complexity. The main result is that, contrary to the classical model, the balance of challenges and skills remains a necessary but not sufficient condition. The level of challenges and skills must be elevated or at any rate must be higher than the subjective mean. Although channel 6 presents a balance between perceived challenges and skills, they are both lower than the subjective mean, and it is therefore characterized by a negative experiential state.

It also seems that subjects are able to organize an experience positively when the situation presents an increase in the complexity of the challenges offered by external contexts. In these cases, the interaction between the internal and external world is organized in an integrated and emergent way, as understood by Csikszentmihalyi in his classification of endogenous motives. The quality of experience here is not preestablished by previous conditions because the individual is able to use skills, cultivated through experience, to face environmental challenges that are even higher than those already faced before.

In such cases, attentional processes become separated from consciousness, which normally regulates attention on the basis of preexisting data. Behavior is then organized around a new experiential nucleus, whose ordered and harmonious composition itself (i.e., the lack of conflict among the various psychic components and between the internal world and external contexts) attracts attention and organizes the experiential state. Contexts that allow for such integrated regulation of the various psychic functions are therefore sought out and repeated, even though they were not part of the subject's motivations up to that point. This constitutes emergent motivation, with the consequent possibility of behavioral development. It should be noted how this "complexification" of challenges and skills, and this uncoupling of the unilateral relationship between consciousness and attention, matches the theoretical remarks presented in the initial sections of this volume.

A further requirement is that the increase of external opportunities has to develop around an existing core, and has to occur in an orderly fashion. In other words, the situation must be congruent with the intrinsic motivations of the subject, and therefore with the innermost parts of his or her identity, which are thus preserved. Consequently, it is necessary for the increase in complexity not to be exceedingly high, so that the subject will be able to integrate the novelty with the information already mastered – information that then goes through a further increase in complexity. From this it follows that the great majority of the information present in external contexts (manifested by the various challenges) and in the internal world (manifested as skills) is replicated through optimal experience, which, for the reasons just mentioned, allows for the introduction of only a small quantity of new information.

This process results in what has been previously described as psychological teleonomy: the regular replication of organization and the introduction of new information in an ordered, negentropic fashion. This occurs both externally (environmental challenges) and internally (the psychic system and its skills). We shall now focus on the latter.

2.4.8 Optimal Experience and the Development of the Self

The view of behavior proposed by Csikszentmihalyi considers the individual and the environment as interacting factors and part of the same open system. This postulate is grounded in a specific view of the self. Csikszentmihalyi claims that

> A self is the information an organism has about its own states. The self is structured around intentions, or goals, which provide an axis for ordering information about itself. Information consists of events in consciousness; thus the self is also a content of consciousness. To select, process, and store information requires the allocation of a finite human resource, namely, attention. (Csikszentmihalyi, 1985, pp.99–100).

In short, according to Csikszentmihalyi, the self is "psychic energy invested in goals" (Csikszentmihalyi, *ibid.*, p.107) both internal and external, and therefore the self grows when the goals on which attention is focused become more complex. Csikszentmihalyi's hypothesis is that flow represents an emergent function of the self close to Mead's I (1934), as already discussed.

The integrated state of flow allows the self to save energy by dispensing with self-observation as a means of regulating its own activity. Full involvement in the action at hand, and the consequent balance with environmental demands, allow one to bypass the cognitive functions that usually mediate personal motivations and environmental rules. Intrinsic motivations and self-determination are instead accessed, in complete agreement with external rules and the demands of social reality. Thus, as Mead claims, that part of the self known to the subject only when it is actively functioning, is free to act. This is the autonomous, aware, and ordered part of the self that Mead defined as the "I."

Once this kind of experience ends, the usual functions of the self resume. Because of the lack of fit between challenges and skills, attention must again be invested in negotiating the relation between the outer and the inner realms. So the functions of the self become those that can be described as objects if observed externally. It is that part of the self defined by Mead as the "Me." But the self that resumes to function after an experience of flow has meanwhile changed. And this is due to various factors.

Flow, as we have seen, is an emergent experience, not mechanically predetermined by information already present in consciousness. It also entails focusing psychic energy on challenges and opportunities for action increasingly more complex. This is due to the evolving aspects of this kind of experience, and in particular, to the fact that channel 1 (challenges slightly higher than skills) is associated with a positive experiential state. To this process is added the development of increasingly complex skills, in agreement with environmental challenges.

The information contained in the self grows through this type of experience. Optimal experience nourishes the self by enriching it in information. After the I has acted, the Me available to be described by consciousness is different, richer and more complex. The self therefore grows as a result of continuous learning, stimulated by freely chosen goals. This same process stimulates the subject to seek out the experience of flow. Flow is the source for the development of the self throughout the life span (Csikszentmihalyi, 1982, 1985, 1990).

2.4.9 Correspondence with Other Theories

The close examination of the theory of flow demonstrates that it is indebted to other perspectives, in particular to certain ideas of James, Mead, and the theoreticians of intrinsic motivation. The theory of optimal experience, as the reader will have noticed, also achieved an original integration of different currents of thought. This integration is achieved as follows.

Let us start from the most recent theory, the one developed by Deci and Ryan regarding intrinsic motivation. In this case, the similarity seems evident, concerning for example, the centrality of the concepts of self-determination and competence, and the necessity itself of intrinsic motivation, in order for the autotelic experience of flow to emerge.

However, the theory of flow is distinct because it is concerned primarily – and from a *methodological* point of view – with the development of psychic processes in real-life contexts. In contrast to the advocates of intrinsic motivation, who elaborate their ideas largely on the basis of studies conducted in laboratories, the Chicago authors tend to go "to the field," using research methods such as the Experience Sampling Method (ESM). The latter aims to provide precise measures of internal states in different real-life contexts. This interest also becomes a *theoretical* one, as we shall see in Chapter 3, in that challenges and external opportunities, and the individual's interaction with them, are not only seen as scenarios in which the individual's behavior develops. They are also seen as the element of a human culture in evolution, elements with which individuals interact in a complex fashion. Individuals, owing to their experiences and to their emergent actions, can bring about significant changes within these very cultural contexts.

Furthermore, with respect to the theory of intrinsic motivation, in the theory of flow there is also a greater interest in the *phenomenology* and organization of experience in all its aspects. The analysis of the cognitive and affective (in addition to the motivational) components is more evident, and the interest in the quality of the subjective state is also greater. If the latter is adequately organized, it stimulates action and behavioral development.

As far as the relationship of flow to the thought of William James is concerned, the debt is more indirect but not less extensive, since it concerns the entire issue of behavior, and, more specifically, the concepts of consciousness and attention. Generally speaking, Csikszentmihalyi is more interested in considering an experience not only with respect to its internal organization (volition, emotion, and cognition, which are fundamental issues in James's thought), but also vis-à-vis its relationships with activities and real-life situations, relationships that are represented by challenges.

Recognizing the fundamental importance of phenomenology, Csikszentmihalyi points out that, in any given society, experiences are culturally marked. In other words, subjects tend to repeat and seek out not only optimal experiences, but also activities associated with them and that allow for the experiences to occur. The characteristics of these activities depend on the surrounding cultural context, and their very repetition and cultivation affect cultural evolutionary processes. The activities and contexts associated with optimal experience will tend to remain constant in that culture and to be transmitted over time.

To conclude, let us return briefly to Mead's thought, and in particular, to his discussion of the development of the self. Again, Csikszentmihalyi's thought differs from Mead in that it focuses on how experience is organized, and on the idea that the constitution and the development of the self derive not only from the interaction with the external social environment, but also from the very structure of consciousness, which can take on emergent characteristics. Furthermore, the evaluation of challenges largely depends on subjective perception and, hence, not exclusively on the actual influence of the social world.

Another difference between the two lines of thought derives from the view that in certain cases challenges, according to Csikszentmihalyi, are internal and not external or social – for instance in situations of "nonaction," as in meditation, contemplation, or solitude, in which the person balances skills with demands coming from his or her consciousness (Delle Fave and Larson, 1993).

2.5 THE AUTOTELIC PERSONALITY

Subsequent studies led to the formulation of a new concept that seems to enlarge the horizon of the theory (Csikszentmihalyi and

90

Nakamura, 1989; Csikszentmihalyi and Rathunde, 1993; Csikszentmihalyi, 1997). Research on the experience of flow suggests that an optimal regulation of life-span development is based on the capacity for achieving, maintaining, and evolving states of optimal experience to increasingly greater levels of complexity. These processes are grounded in the capacity of structuring interactions with the environment according to modalities facilitating flow.

To this end, the main requirements, which can be called *metaskills* (Csikszentmihalyi and Nakamura, 1989) include:

1. The capacity to focus attention on the situation at hand by maintaining high levels of concentration

2. Clear definition of one's own aims with respect to the situation at hand and the identification of the necessary and available means for achieving them

3. The capacity to look for adequate feedback in the situation and to associate it with one's own aims and motivations

4. The capacity to continuously modulate both the subjective perception and the actual level of balance between challenges and skills

This last process takes place by using unbalanced states of anxiety and boredom as information to identify the sources that could lead to an increase in skills (in the case of anxiety), or to find new and more complex challenges (in the case of boredom, or in the case of a general increase of skills). With respect to these issues, the ability to tolerate with a certain ease anxiety-provoking interactions seems particularly relevant.

Another very important metaskill is the capacity to delay immediate gratification in order to gradually cultivate situations and activities requiring an extended investment of energy before producing significant intrinsic rewards (Csikszentmihalyi and Nakamura, 1989).

The individual who has such basic resources, or metaskills, seems to be more effective in the environment, in reaching positive experiences, and in developing a more complete self by facing new challenges. Such a person is also more likely to discover new social contexts in which to act. This set of personal characteristics is fundamental to the growth of the individual and to the possibility of making a positive contribution to the development of the social contexts to which one belongs.

Given the relevance of these factors, it is important to determine the source of individual differences in these metaskills; and further, whether they are stable traits of a person or whether they depend on the specific interactions in which the person is involved at different moments. Csikszentmihalyi (1988b) therefore introduces the concept of *autotelic personality*.

As previously mentioned, the term *autotelic* refers to noninstrumental experiences and activities that are not primarily motivated by external or future rewards; activities done for their own sake, where the action is experienced as rewarding in itself because it is connected with the person's internal motivations.

An autotelic personality is characterized by the tendency to find intrinsic motivation and to experience flow in daily life. The autotelic individual is able to discover optimal (i.e., integrated and complex) experiences in situations that others might tend to consider boring or a source of anxiety (Csikszentmihalyi, 1990). Autotelic persons are more complex, responding in a less predetermined way to environmental demands. In fact they are able to regulate their own state of arousal. They are able to control and modulate their behavior even when the environmental demands are exceedingly high, or when their skills are insufficient. Conversely, they are capable of discovering new environmental stimuli and taking risks when the external challenges are lacking or when the skills are too high (Csikszentmihalyi and Rathunde, 1993).

Autotelic persons are therefore able to develop emergent motivations by looking for new and more complex challenges, and also to show their self-determination by withdrawing from overly unbalanced situations, or by reinterpreting these situations in order to reinsert them into their own goals (in line with the concept of integrated and self-determined extrinsic motivation proposed by Deci and Ryan, 1985).

By the end of the 1980s, research had been directed to the understanding of a possible correlation between the specific characteristics of external contexts and the development in a child of this type of personality. Researchers have been focusing their attention in particular on environmental stimuli – above all, the family – that might lead to the development of these skills (Rathunde, 1988, 1989; Csikszentmihalyi and Rathunde, 1998).

There are numerous theories that could furnish a starting point for this discussion. Csikszentmihalyi's and his collaborators' effort was, first of all, to point out the possible connections between existing theories of child development and the concept of autotelic personality. They have primarily taken into consideration the capacity for behavioral modulation, which seems to be a central component of this type of personality.

It is therefore useful to analyze theories that show the positive role of the family environment (in the development of the personality) characterized by an alternation of, and a balance between, the two poles represented respectively by a stimulating and a supporting situation. The necessity of balancing these two poles is central in Freudian thought. The negotiation between instincts and reality is what brings about an integrated development of the Ego. In this process also, the ability of the Ego to negotiate is influenced by overly indulgent or restrictive strategies employed by parental figures during the various developmental phases (Freud, 1932).

Similarly, theories of optimal arousal claim that the alternation between an increase and a decrease of environmental stimuli leads to an optimal situation. The growth of the self, according to this theory, derives from a dialectic tension between levels of high and low arousal (Berlyne, 1960; Fiske and Maddi, 1961; Apter, 1989).

Of particular interest to the analysis of the formation of the autotelic personality is also, according to Rathunde and Csikszentmihalyi (1991), the attempt to connect the theories of optimal arousal with attachment theories. On this line of research, we shall consider the discussion of the mother–child interaction proposed by Bowlby (1969). Field (1985) suggests that attachment between mother and child, as between two individuals in general, is based on mutual stimulation (which is to say, the possibility for exploring, discovering, and finding out what's new) and support (which is to say, the possibility for understanding). According to Isabella and Belsky (1991) both understimulation and ovestimulation from the mother disturbs the affective bond. It is also known that the child needs security and support in order to feel pleasure and in order to explore through play (Ainsworth, Bell and Stayton, 1971). Later studies (Grotevant and Cooper, 1983; Rathunde and Csikszentmihalyi, 1991) suggest that also during adolescence it is the very condition of reassuring dependence that allows for original discovery of the environment and for risk taking. These studies also point out the positive role of the two sustaining poles of support and stimulation.

Also, Baumrind's discussion (1989) of the concept of authoritative parenting style can be thought of as falling along these lines. This parenting style characterizes parents who are in turn exigent and appreciative – offering a familial environment neither overly permissive nor overly rigid, and therefore favorable to the optimal development of the child and to the training of the child's competence.

These theories, therefore, point out the positive role in the development of the personality played by the dialectic tension between two opposed and complementary poles, the first including indulgence, generosity, and support, and the other boundaries, expectations, and behavioral requirements. Csikszentmihalyi and Rathunde (1993) point out that these two poles both support personal skills and increase environmental demands in the exact way proposed by the theory of flow. A family characterized by this complementarity might stimulate the child to develop an adequate balance between challenges and skills, and to face anxiety or boredom while reaching a good behavioral modulation between security and search for new contexts of action.

Starting from these theoretical presuppositions and on the basis of specific research instruments (such as the Complex Family Questionnaire) Csikszentmihalyi and Rathunde (1993) suggest two fundamental types of familial dimensions, styles, or climates. These are characterized by integration and differentiation, respectively.

Generally speaking, a family having an integrated relational style tends to encourage in the child concentration, seriousness, a clear direction toward external aims, and emotional well-being. This type of family also encourages economizing attention resources thanks to the sense of security and organization that such a family provides. Conversely, a family characterized by differentiation stimulates in the child the desire to explore, ambition, and the possibility to autonomously exert his or her own skills with the aim of pursuing goals perceived as unique and personal.

A familial context is autotelic when it alternates instances of integration and differentiation. In such cases, we can speak of a complex family (Rathunde and Csikszentmihalyi, 1991; Csikszentmihalyi and Rathunde, 1993, 1998).

A balanced dialectic between these two poles is then internalized by the child. The latter will be able to face new contexts, sustained by a reassuring internal condition. This possibility of experiencing integration and differentiation within the family tends to lead to greater flexibility in behavioral regulation. Integration in the family presents children with challenges characterized by security and support. Differentiation creates an environment rich in stimulations, allowing children to define themselves not only autonomously, but also taking into consideration the characteristics and conditions posed by other members of the family. Thus, the combination of these two dimensions offers the possibility to face in an articulated way feelings of boredom and anxiety, and to develop a complex personality able to face environmental challenges without neglecting one's own deep motivations.

The data reported by Csikszentmihalyi and Rathunde (1993), and in particular Rathunde (1993) and Hektner (1996), seem to suggest that the correlation existing between complex families and autotelic personality provides children with a stable personality trait. This is most evident in academic settings, where these authors find a significant correlation between complex families, autotelic personality, and academic achievement (Csikszentmihalyi and Rathunde, 1993, 1998; Rathunde, 1993; Huang, 1997). Autotelic personality seems, therefore, to be a stable trait.

In short, the autotelic personality is formed within the integrated relationship between environmental challenges and personal skills found at first in daily family life, and subsequently in social contexts. Therefore, children will tend to acquire the capacity to face moments of boredom and anxiety by modulating their own behavior in situations protected, in a certain sense, by familial conditions. They will achieve optimal experience by fully employing their own competencies and skills. They will build a complex self able to support them throughout the life span, leading to a continuous development of the personality.

3

SUBJECTIVE EXPERIENCE
AND SOCIAL CONTEXTS

I N THIS, THE THIRD AND FINAL CHAPTER, WE SHALL UNDERTAKE
the analysis of three themes, which describe alternative ways of
applying to specific settings the theoretical concepts discussed
thus far. If until now we have considered subjective experience
from the point of view of its optimal configuration, subjective
experience can also organize itself in a disturbed fashion. For
instance, anxiety, boredom, and apathy represent times at which
consciousness is not harmoniously regulated.

In the first section of this chapter, we shall discuss conditions
under which this regulation fails in a serious way. We shall therefore tackle the problem of mental disturbance and psychopathology. In the second section, we shall explore the opposite case: we
shall speak of some of these theories' suggestions regarding creative processes in real-life contexts. Finally, in the third section, we
shall focus on daily mechanisms of cultural evolution and their
relation to states of subjective experience. This section represents a
starting point for the analysis of the general mechanisms through
which individuals develop their personalities and, at the same
time, through which human cultures are transmitted over time.

We shall place ourselves, once more, in the vast current of contemporary psychology that studies normal human beings in their
daily existence.

3.1 QUALITY OF EXPERIENCE
AND MENTAL HEALTH

3.1.1 Mental Disturbance as Psychic Entropy

We have pointed out several times that each individual internalizes daily part of the surrounding external culture by being in

97

contact with the group to which he or she belongs. Family and academic environment – to which today we can increasingly add the relationship with peers and the mass media – represent the two primary instances of socialization and development of what we can define as intrasomatic culture, which is to say, culture deposited within the individual (Cloack, 1975).

Such internalization occurs by means of countless instances of subjective experience in real-life contexts. As we shall see more clearly in the third section of this chapter, this is a physiological mechanism through which the subject's identity is formed and through which, at the same time, the existing cultural information is maintained or modified. We shall also see that this takes place due to the ability of real-life contexts to attract the motivational, cognitive, and affective interest of people. When this occurs, individuals identify themselves with norms, values, and cultural lifestyles, while internalizing and transmitting them over time. By means of this process, a cultural network is formed within the mind and connected in different degrees to the external cultural network of the society to which these individuals belong (Massimini and Calegari, 1979; Terranova-Cecchini, 1985; Massimini, Terranova-Cecchini and Inghilleri, 1985; Nathan, 1986; Berry, Poortinga, Segall and Dasen, 1992).

Each one of us sees oneself as being more or less in harmony with the external network. Mental health or illness is related to this variability and degree of harmony, and their cognitive and affective components. Psychic disturbance can occur in all situations in which psychic teleonomy and its integration with biological and cultural teleonomies are not realized. In other words, there are life courses in which people are rarely able to increase the complexity of internal and social information – that is, to express themselves or produce original changes. In other cases, individuals are not able to retrace known and familiar paths – that is, to achieve the ordered repetition of stable and integrated information.

Psychic disturbances can therefore be seen as the result of the inability to focus psychic energy on the contexts offered by society, and of the subsequent decline in the quality of subjective experience. In particular, and on the basis of the theory of flow, situations that produce an excessive and repeated imbalance between challenges and skills are especially at risk. This can occur in different contexts, all crucial for the development of a human being: in the family, in academic and working environments, in the relationship between an individual and the norms and values of his or her culture, and in the relationship with one's own internal world. All of these situations are deeply interconnected in real life.

Let us consider, for instance, complex families characterized by an alternation of normative strategies and strategies aimed at developing personal autonomy. If a family environment provides only one of these two polarities – continuous demands and strictness, or a permissive situation lacking challenges – the child is immersed, respectively, in repeated states of anxiety or boredom and might not develop a flexible personality. This mechanism can become even more well rooted if the more extended extra-familial social environment shows the same imbalance. Such children will therefore tend to develop insufficiently their self-esteem, knowledge of their identities and skills, and confidence in the possibility to positively interact with the social world. All of this implies a scarcity of integrated subjective experience, and therefore a sort of constraint of the personality, together with the tendency to direct oneself toward contexts and challenges that in some way still allow the individual to have something like an integrated experience.

This situation of deep and disturbing imbalance between an individual's internal world and the demands of the social world can occur not only within the family, but also in other contexts, such as the academic or the work environment. In the last few years there has been an animated discussion concerning ways to improve the quality of academic and work performance, and this often only with the aim of optimizing the productivity of academic institutions or of firms. Less attention seems to have been devoted to the students or workers, and to the prevention of psychic suffering and disturbance that in some cases affect youngsters and adults in their daily experiences of studying or working. We shall not tackle this problem extensively here, but we shall attempt to define possible general situations of psychic entropy.

3.1.2 Psychic Disorder as Exclusion
from the Cultural Network

This issue can be approached from four different angles:

1. The progressive separation of the individual from the surrounding social reality has been defined by some authors as "marginalization"[1] (Massimini, Terranova-Cecchini and Inghilleri, 1985; Massimini, Csikszentmihalyi and Carli, 1987). As already mentioned at the beginning of this chapter, culture can be viewed as a network of behavioral instructions deposited in the external world and available to the individual to be internalized. When individuals find themselves on the outside of the cultural network, they are in a situation of marginalization.

2. There are two forms of marginalization. Although they both share the final result, meaning the progressive separation of an individual from the cultural reality in which he or she lives, they derive from two distinct paths that make them radically different.

3. The first form of marginalization can be defined as "voluntary," in that it derives, at least initially, from behavioral strategies actively selected by the subject. This form can, in turn, be distinguished into two types. In the first type, the subject addresses voluntarily his or her own psychic energy toward cultural opportunities that are either partially or completely different from the ones held by the majority of the population. Because of past experiences, only in this way will the individual be able to have a positive, complex, and negentropic experience. Studies regarding so-called "neovagrantism" show, for instance, that, at least in Italy, some homeless individuals freely choose to depart from the prevailing social rules by following lifestyles that allow them to organize their experience in an essentially positive way (Delle Fave, Massimini and Maletto, 1991a).

Another example of this form of marginalization is represented by the formation of youth groups or gangs having autonomous rules, symbols, and behaviors (see, for instance, Sato, 1988). In this case, the specific reality of this subculture provides the challenges that the subjects perceive as being balanced with and stimulating for their own skills, often as opposed to the challenges offered by the adult world. Thus, a progressive focus of psychic processes toward the rules of the alternative groups or cultures occurs. The latter are the only ones allowing these young people, at least for a brief period of time, to have a positive experience.

A third example, in a way more hidden and complex, is offered by the voluntary form of marginalization realized by the very activation of a psychopathological symptom. We can think of those behaviors increasingly less connected to external values and more introversive, or of openly pathological behaviors such as obsessive rituals, phobias, or even delirious behaviors. These, although pathological, can provide the subject with an internal condition in which, artificially and subjectively, challenges and skills are perceived as balanced, and in which the individual experiences intrinsic motivation and stimulates his or her cognitive state. But such an organization of the psychic apparatus, which structurally corresponds to the experience that we have defined as optimal, is directed toward challenges far from the ones shared by the majority of the population or from the demands of adaptation to reality. The individual, in order to reach an organized experiential state, creates his or her own pathology. The psychiatric symptom then represents the attempt to experience, at least in fantasy, a balance between internal capacities and external demands. In other words, the subject creates, at the level of fantasy, an at-times complete transformation of the external world. By means of this transformation, he or she reorganizes an image of his or her own internal organization that belongs only to him or her and that therefore does not allow for any real relationship with the external world. We are therefore speaking here of an extreme and fruitless attempt to reach psychic order that instead opens the way only to suffering and illness.

The same ruinous path is shared by the other two forms of voluntary marginalization already mentioned. They initially allow individuals to reach a positive experience by means of choosing different lifestyles or by means of closing themselves up in the rules of an alternative group. The psychic energy of the individual will therefore be directed more and more toward these styles and rules. But such mechanisms imply that it will be increasingly

101

difficult to obtain an integrated experience through contacts with the cultural reality of the majority and its challenges. An individual's skills are, in fact, more and more cultivated exclusively within the social niche in which he or she decides to live. The cultural network of the majority becomes foreign, distant, and overly demanding. The subject then tends to separate him or herself even more from it and to experience entropic psychological states and suffering every time he or she has to face the tests or the demands of the "normality:" Thus, psychic deviance and disturbance emerge.

4. There exists, then, a second form of marginalization that we might call forced. In certain cases the discrepancy between the internal and external network, and the impossibility for some individuals to invest their own significant experiences in real social contexts, derive from precise social situations characterized by exclusion. In cases of forced marginalization, individuals are excluded from social challenges in a compulsory way. Extreme examples of this situation are prisons or psychiatric hospitals completely closed off from the external world and lacking any rehabilitating activity. These institutions segregate individuals and block their development. It is impossible for them to access social opportunities and make use of their own skills.

Marginalization can also occur in other instances of forced social isolation, sometimes present within the very family of origin, or more often due to economical or social factors. Individuals in these situations are prevented from using their skills in stimulating contexts. In certain cases, the external contexts do not even present a minimum level of complexity in order for social action to occur. Consequently, a behavioral contraction and closure are present, like the ones taken into consideration in the first type of marginalization.

Since the 1960s, important authors in social psychiatry have pointed out that psychiatric illness can derive from specific family dynamics, due to which individuals are unable to develop their own potentials and express their own motivations, up to the point of separating themselves completely from reality (Laing and Esterson, 1964). This approach is still followed and can be found more recently in more specific sectors of psychiatry. A careful review of the literature on Post Traumatic Stress Disorder (Wilson and Raphael, 1993) allows for the recognition that one of the most severe and common consequences of such events is the persisting perception of the impossibility of utilizing one's own skills and of autonomously directing oneself toward chosen aims. It is as if the initial traumatic event made the individual incapable of feeling integrated with the demands required, and the opportunities offered, by an external world that has in the past presented overly elevated, violent, and incomprehensible challenges for the individual.

This extreme situation is an example of a series of more or less severe events in which at any rate the family or social situation persistently does not allow the individual to experience a balance between challenges and skills and to develop him or herself. At times this occurs for specific economic or social reasons. The individuals who, due to these causes, are denied access to academic, working, or even freely chosen or recreational opportunities, toward which they are internally motivated or which they might want to cultivate, find themselves in a severe situation of marginalization. The latter does not open the way to psychic complexity and can easily lead them along a path of disorder, psychic entropy, and disturbance. We can for instance think of those more marginalized children and youngsters of many developing countries. But this socially disadvantaged situation, which becomes a disadvantage as far as psychological growth is concerned, concerns also large portions of youngsters in developed countries, in particular when they belong to ethnic minorities or disadvantaged portions of the population.

Even in cases of forced marginalization, the individual can initially attempt to artificially rebuild a situation simulating psychic integration. But even here we are speaking of a pathological behavior. The symptoms, which can manifest themselves in actions, cognition, or affectivity, represent anomalous or fantastic ways of balancing one's skills and external challenges. This balance is purely subjective and is in fact disconnected from normal values, rules, and social categories. It will therefore not succeed and it will reveal itself to be only a sign of psychic entropy.

103

3.1.3 The Restoration of Psychic Order

Our theoretical discussion allows us to hypothesize a general mechanism that might be at the origin of psychic disturbance, and to define a therapeutic and rehabilitating program. The latter must be based on three main lines of action.

First of all, we have to identify the cases of forced marginalization related to the family, social, or possibly the psychiatric history of the subject. We are speaking here of pointing out the possible negative past or present actions exerted by factors or structures causing the marginalization, and of progressively closing them up or transforming them.

Second, we need to highlight the original mechanism underlying the disturbance of each single patient. This analysis is carried out by using the level of progressive separation between the internal world, with its skills, and the external world, with its challenges, as an interpretative grid. In this process we need to take into consideration that this imbalance is due to specific family or social situations, or to mechanisms forcing a separation from the cultural network, as, for instance, a long stay in a mental hospital or in prison.

Finally, it will be necessary to identify the remaining ability of the patient to achieve optimal experience in real-life contexts. We shall then start from this very ability, which can be found in every individual, even when very degenerated, in order to develop a rehabilitating project that can lead the patient to face increasingly more complex challenges connected to more complex social elements. In this way the individual will progressively reconstitute his or her internal culture and identity through a positive relationship with the social context.

This last point can be developed through several phases:

1. It is necessary to offer the patient more complex challenges (by which I mean also interpersonal relationships) with respect to the ones that he or she currently faces daily in institutions or even more frequently in the family.

2. These environmental challenges have to be real and related to the surrounding social network.

3. The rehabilitation needs to be highly personalized and needs to respect the characteristics of the single individual. Only in this way will the latter be able to freely select challenges and to experience a sense of autonomy while going through this process with his or her actual skills, thus avoiding dangerous unbalancing situations.

4. The activities and relationships proposed need to be complex, proportionally to the specific situation of the patient. Only in this way will the latter be able gradually to improve his or her own skills. On the other hand, repetitive or overly simple activities obstruct the dynamic process of development of optimal experience and of the personality.

5. Each patient tends to autonomously associate certain activities with optimal experience and therefore needs to be helped to cultivate those activities, which is to say, to invest more and more of his or her cognition, motivation, and emotions on them, discovering in an original way new challenges (Massimini and Delle Fave, 1988).

On the basis of this theoretical perspective new psychiatric interventions have been developed both in Western countries, for instance in France and Italy, and in those belonging to the so-called third world, such as Nicaragua and Northern Somalia. In Nicaragua, in particular, an important part of the reorganization of the local psychiatric services followed this perspective in the 1980s.

Although we refer the interested reader to the specific literature concerned with this issue (Inghilleri, 1986; Terranova-Cecchini and Panzeri, 1986), we shall nevertheless mention some of the crucial aspects of this endeavor. Two important steps have been the progressive emptying of the central psychiatric hospital located in Managua, in order to avoid further cases of marginalization, and the protected relocation of the patients in their families and original communities. This relocation has been facilitated by the strong social solidarity present in that Central-American country, especially in those years.

Another fundamental aspect was the opening of social centers where the inhabitants of an area could meet and where at the same time the patients living in these communities could benefit from therapeutic activities. In these social centers various activities are available: academic activities, reading, the construction of artifacts and their marketing, and small-scale agriculture. In this way, gradually and in a controlled fashion, patients are reintegrated into different real-life domains. The latter are autonomously selected by these patients in the very place where they occur and interact with the more extended social network.

Another crucial aspect was to bring the more serious patients to perform such activities as the harvesting of coffee – traditionally one of the most well-known and practiced source of working and social identity for the Nicaraguan population. Highly disturbed patients who in certain cases had been residents in a mental hospital for many years were made able to perform an activity they hadn't conducted in years but that was once known to them – for instance, the harvesting of coffee. These patients rapidly exhibited an increase in their motor skills, which had been considered lost. Most of all, they were able to experience a positive and integrated state of consciousness that they had not experienced in years. Experiencing one's own skills in connection with part of an almost entirely lost past identity has, in many cases, opened the way to a progressive enhancement of both personal skills and environmental challenges, supported by positive subjective experience. The latter seems to be the very source of the rehabilitating process.

An important aspect of this theoretical approach is, in a certain way, its "transportability" from one culture to another. Personal skills and environmental challenge are universal concepts that concern all human beings. Each person and each human culture can then idiosyncratically and specifically define what will be the relevant challenges and skills active in a given context. Therefore, the psychiatric methodology that we have described in brief and general terms is applicable in very different cultural situations. For instance, an active program at the Barbera's Mental Hospital

(Northern Somalia) follows this approach. The latter has been developed in a rather different way from the Nicaraguan's example and respects the native culture. The law of the Koran, the clans' and tribes' rules, the family norms, the ways in which the genders are organized in that context, the means of subsistence, and the traditional healing practices all represent specific scenarios in which, in that specific culture, the relationship between challenges and skills and the development or the obtrusion of psychic complexity are located, and with respect to which the therapeutic practices are organized (Inghilleri, 1997).

The application in psychiatry of the theories of subjective experience and of the procedures connected with them are also widely developed in Western countries (DeVries, 1992). In recent years the theory of flow and self-determination have been applied, in the clinical domain, to psychotherapeutic practice. The use of specific methods of research of daily experience, such as the previously mentioned Experience Sampling Method (ESM), allowed the measuring and evaluation of experiential and emotional responses to psychotherapeutic action (Delle Fave and Massimini, 1992; Massimini, Inghilleri and Delle Fave, 1996).

The ESM is given to patients at the beginning of the therapy and is used as a diagnostic instrument to identify the activities, contexts, and thought contents that in daily life bring the subjects to experience negative states of anxiety, boredom, apathy, or positive states of flow or self-determination. Thus, we obtain a profile of the patients on which to base a therapeutic strategy leading to the development of a greater awareness of the reasons of their difficulties and of the contexts triggering them, on the one hand, and, on the other, of those rare situations that instead facilitate integrated experiences. At the same time, of course, the actual encounter with the therapist is used as an opportunity to experiment with the possibility of perceiving in a protected way the imbalance between external demands and internal skills, of confronting this imbalance (thus creating an ordered and integrated experience), and of then facing the risk of new challenges.

The ESM is then used to monitor the patients' progress. The ways in which subjects modulate their own internal organization

107

in function of environmental demands, and in which they do or do not have optimal and integrated experiences, are evaluated at regular intervals – for instance one week-long screening (of daily experiences) every two months (Hurlburt, 1990; Delle Fave and Massimini, 1992; Csikszentmihalyi and Rathunde, 1993).

To conclude, these recent studies seem to point out once more the importance of subjective experience in processes of individual change carried out in close connection with the various contexts of life. The existence of a specific theory concerning subjective experience and of adequate means of inquiry allows us to individuate a line of research that might not only confirm or further develop these theoretical constructs, but might also help to develop useful interventive strategies in clinical and therapeutic settings.

3.2 SUBJECTIVE EXPERIENCE AND CREATIVITY

We shall now approach a topic that lies at the opposite side of the spectrum with respect to the one considered up to this point, namely, the relationships between subjective experience, personality, and creativity. By the latter we understand a basic process of psychic functioning which concerns all individuals (Gardner, 1983; 1993).

For several years the subject of creativity has constituted an important branch of general psychology and it has also been of interest to studies concerned with "problem solving" and "problem finding" (Simon, 1988; Sternberg, 1988; Csikszentmihalyi, 1988a, 1996). To define intelligence, not only as the ability to solve problems, but also as the capacity to find or create problems (Gardner, 1983), contributes to inserting creativity into the domain of basic human competencies found in the most diverse contexts of daily life.

In addition, studies of human cultural evolution and individual psychological selection point out – as mentioned in earlier sections of this volume – the mutually determining relationship between the processes of transmission and transformation of cultural information deposited in extra-individual loci on the one hand, and the quality and the structure of an individual's psychic processes (among which we count creativity) on the other. Therefore, creativity has to be understood as the result of various influences and not merely as a process internal to the individual.

The discussion has therefore widened to include the relationship between creative and social processes. The question "What is creativity?" is gradually substituted with the question "Where is creativity?" (Csikszentmihalyi, 1988a, 1996). In order to answer this question, we will employ a series of brief definitions.

3.2.1 The Elements of Creativity

The first element of creativity is a symbolic system, or *domain:* We shall define as a symbolic system that portion of material culture (Cloack, 1975), or in different terms, of extrasomatic culture (Massimini and Inghilleri, 1993), to which the creative work connects itself and whose structure lies at the basis of the possibility of an individual to find new solutions to known problems or to find new problems.

An example of a symbolic system (Csikszentmihalyi, 1988a) is "the state of the art" at a given historical time, of a scientific or artistic discipline, or of a normative system on which the artist, the scientist, or the legislator respectively act. Each specific "state of the art" derives from a historical process of cultural evolution. Such a process is strictly connected to mechanisms of individual psychological selection and to their respective experiential states.

The second element of creativity is the *individual:* The second force at play in creative processes is represented by the single individual who, with his or her thoughts and behaviors, is able to produce a change in a symbolic system. This change is considered creative if and when it is accepted by the field, or the set of social forces involved in that domain.

The large literature on this topic has been systematized long ago, primarily according to three levels:[2]

1. The quality of subjective experience that lies at the basis of and accompanies the creative process: the state of optimal experience or flow is a good model of this (Csikszentmihalyi, 1988a, 1996)
2. Basic competencies and potential, both biological and cognitive (for an exhaustive literature review regarding this subject, see Gardner, 1988b, 1993)
3. Motivations for creativity (see Amabile, 1983)

We shall now briefly discuss the last two of these three levels, putting aside the concept of optimal experience, which has already been discussed in this volume.

As far as the cognitive approaches are concerned, the concept of *multiple intelligence* developed by Gardner (1983) is particularly interesting. This concept has been further developed by the same author at later times (Gardner, 1988a, 1993).[3] In short, we can say that Gardner initially defines a finite number of criteria by means of whose satisfaction a set of intellectual abilities can be defined as a certain type of intelligence. We thus find eight criteria: (1) the isolation of faculties as a result of brain damage; (2) the functions present in "idiots savants," prodigies, and other exceptional individuals; (3) the possibility of identifying central mechanisms that process specific information; (4) a distinctive history of ontogenetic development; (5) the presence of a plausible or specific evolutionary (phylogenetic) history; (6) the proofs provided by psychological tests, which are the object of experimental studies; (7) the proofs provided by psychometric results; (8) the susceptibility to encoding in a specific system of symbols (Gardner, 1993, p.63–66).

By analyzing an enormous quantity of bibliographical material, Gardner comes to define the following types of intelligence: (1) linguistic; (2) musical; (3) logical-mathematical; (4) spatial; (5) bodily-kinesthetic; (6) personal, which in turn is divided into intra-personal and (7) inter-personal. Each individual is predisposed in different degrees to these cognitive skills, which have both a cognitive and neural basis. These skills are then developed through interaction with the environment.

It seems obvious that an individual's creative processes are, according to this view, strictly connected to basic predispositions and to the possibility of using specific types of intelligence (which can be defined as *skills*) in their respective environmental contexts and cognitive tasks (in other words, in opportunities for action and in external *challenges*). We should also note that more recently Gardner himself (1988b, 1993) has integrated his original view with a perspective that takes into consideration the concept of optimal experience and the fact that creativity cannot be reduced solely to the individual.

As far as the motivational aspects of creativity are concerned, we shall refer the reader to the concepts of emergent, intrinsic, and extrinsic motivation, and their different levels of self-determination discussed earlier. However, we shall now briefly discuss certain psychoanalytic views concerning the motivation for creativity. Psychoanalysis has devoted itself to the study of the deep dynamics underlying creative processes. Freud's original perspective viewed artistic and scientific production, and creativity in general, as the expression of an unsatisfied wish. In the case of Leonardo, for instance, the libido is sublimated according to Freud into the desire for knowledge: The sexual instinctual forces are displaced through different aims (Freud, 1910). Later, the relationship between the conscious or preconscious representations supported by secondary processes, and the unconscious representations and instincts supported by primary processes was further elaborated by Ego-psychology (Hartmann, 1958; Kris, 1952). These authors point out the functional autonomy of the Ego. The latter is not considered as much the result of the Id or the mediator between the instincts and the demands of external reality as it is an adaptive psychic agent which autonomously develops its potential, manifesting itself, for instance, in the creative process.

Not far from this perspective is Arieti's contribution (1976). Arieti further discusses the cognitive organizational aspects found at the basis of the particular integration of primary and secondary processes characterizing creative thought and defined as tertiary processes.

111

An interesting aspect of this evolution of psychoanalytic thought is the fact that its analysis of deep motivations for creativity seems to be able to integrate, and not contradict, studies on the other aspects of an individual's level of creativity itself, which is to say, the cognitive elements, intrinsic and integrated extrinsic motivation, and the phenomenology of optimal experience. All of these factors taken together form the individual's side of the creative process, within the different levels of biological and cognitive predisposition, of motivational organization and the quality of the experiential state.

According to Csikszentmihalyi (1988a, 1996), in order to better understand the characteristics of the creative process we need to expand the observation and discussion from the pure domain of an individual's internal world to the complex relationship with the external cultural reality to which the creative elaboration connects itself. Therefore, we shall return to this element of the creative process. We have previously defined the extra-individual culture as the symbolic system inherited by the individual, and in a certain sense available to him or her, on which the creative act depends while being at the same time modified by it. However, we are not speaking of a neutral or nonspecific relationship: The individual in his or her relationship with the symbolic system meets specific social forces active in that part of the culture in which he or she develops the innovative process. We shall now tackle this issue.

The third element of creativity is the social organization of the symbolic system or *field:* The social organization of the symbolic system is that portion of the social system and its members that selects and makes sure that the variations produced by the creative processes are preserved in the cultural memory. The first entity that regulates this process within the life cycle is the family. The latter can favor or obstruct, in a direct or indirect way, the initial creative production of young people. But the main action of the field is developed most of all through institutional or individual forces controlling the discipline involved in the process. In the case of the artist there are critics, customers, colleagues, collectors, and art theoreticians. In the case of the scientist we should instead take into consideration organizations handling grants, academic structures, editors of scientific publications, and the industries or institutions interested in the application of the research results. In the case of a manager, the social organization involved in the process is constituted, for instance, by higher directors, by those who define the basic elements of the "firm culture," by the users of the product resulting from that specific managerial activity, and so on.

Examples of the effect of the social organization of the symbolic system on the development of creativity are various. Csikszentmihalyi (1988a), for instance, mentions the case of Botticelli and Mendel. For centuries Botticelli had been considered not a very refined painter, and the women drawn by him were called "sickly" and "clumsy." Only in the mid-nineteenth century did critics start revaluing his work as a precursor of modern sensibility. The full understanding of the work of Botticelli is due to the analysis of critics such as Ruskin. So much so that, according to Csikszentmihalyi, the study of these authors seems to be as essential to the establishment of the creativity of the artist as much as the expressive work of art itself.

Mendel's fundamental experiments go back approximately to 1860, while his creativity was recognized only 40 years later once the evolutionists, while searching for a mechanism able to explain "discontinuous heredity," "discovered" the crucial importance of the natural selection theory proposed by Mendel. It seems, therefore, that Botticelli's and Mendel's creativity are inseparable from the interpretations of, respectively, Ruskin and the evolutionists of this century. Where, then, does the creativity of this artist or scientist lie? In their minds, in the experiments or works of art, or in the use of the results obtained by them? The answer seems to be: at all three levels (Csikszentmihalyi, 1988a).

Another example of the essential role played by social organization in the development of creativity is offered by Gardner (1988a) in his study on Freud. The author begins by describing the characteristics of Vienna in the second half of last century. In this city there was a tension between social and political conservatism, and an unspoken support for the development of new ideas in the arts and sciences. It was an apparently cohesive society, centered around Catholic and bourgeois values, that was, in fact, cosmopolitan and open to the confrontation of ideas coming from different disciplines. The young Viennese were therefore in the privileged position of being able to critically revise the symbolic systems of the culture to which they were dedicating their interests and energy. Freud was among these youngsters and found himself at the center of diverse cultural influences: He entered areas belonging to the human sciences with a scientific education; he found himself living in a conservative social environment while having fundamentally liberal ideas; he was a Jew in an essentially anti-Semitic society; he was an explorer of sexual dynamics in a "puritan" world. Freud's discoveries derive, in part, from this external situation characterized by this series of polarities. Gardner analyzes this fact through a schema that looks at Freud in his relationship with his family, with his academic environment, with the university and the medical school, with his post-doctoral training in both Paris and Vienna, with the clinics and the private practices in which he made his fundamental observations, with the reviews that published his writings, with the journals where his theories were criticized and at times even ridiculed, with his group of students that met every Wednesday night, with the increasingly larger circle of colleagues, students and patients, and so on. All these elements taken together represent what we have defined as the social organization of the symbolic system on which Freud performed his great transformations.

On the basis of what has been said thus far, we can perhaps now answer our initial question: not merely "What is creativity?" but moreover, "Where is creativity?" Creativity is a complex phenomenon that does not reside exclusively in the individual, but that is developed in three places: (1) the symbolic system of a given cultural area; (2) the social organization of this area; and (3) the individual's psychological processes. These three factors are in a mutually determining relationship: from their interaction the creative process is born.

In order to further clarify this view we shall analyze, as an example, a hypothetical innovative process in biomedical science.

We shall then relate this process to the theoretical concepts proposed in this volume.

The social forces (or field) regulating this system of knowledge are the pharmaceutical companies, the editorial committees of scientific reviews, the administrators of the institutions distributing research grants, the directors of the institutions involved in the experimental processes, and the consumers with their own views on medications and illnesses. On the opposite side we find a relatively precise system of knowledge (or domain), proper to medicine and the biological sciences, concerning the functioning of the human organism and the effect of medications on biological processes.

This is the symbolic system to which the creative process will connect itself. For the latter to take place it is necessary that a person invest one's motivations and skills, both personal and scientific, formed throughout one's life, on cognitive challenges concerning the biomedical symbolic system, balanced with one's skills. But it is also necessary for the institutions regulating the research and its applications to allow the scientists to make use of their skills by making available adequate scientific structures, whether a laboratory or other sites for clinical experimentation. If this occurs the researchers will tend to develop, day after day, optimal subjective experiences by facing the demands and the challenges of the research. They will be then able to fully develop their potential and derive intrinsic rewards and a positive experiential state. The properties of psychological teleonomy will be satisfied.

In this way the development of the complexity of the symbolic system will also be realized. In fact, the researchers will be able to step toward more complex challenges in the area of their referential cultural system (such as biomedical knowledge.) This process will allow researchers to arrive at a new discovery or innovation, subsequently satisfying the properties of cultural teleonomy.

3.2.2 The Development of Creativity

The quality of the interaction between the three elements of creativity has been further investigated by various authors. Some of

115

these underline the necessity of a harmonious and synchronized relationship between these elements in order for the development of life and creative work to occur (see for example the concept of "coincidence" of such factors that brings about innovations, according to Feldman, 1986). For other authors (Gardner, 1988b; Gardner and Wolf, 1988; Csikszentmihalyi, 1996), creativity seems to emerge more easily in the presence of discordance, tension, or "asynchrony" between the different levels considered – for example, when particular types of intelligence and individual motivations are unusual and are in conflict with the cultural milieu of the time and the social forces regulating it at a given historical moment.

The theoretical discussion characterizing these approaches to creativity suggests ways for allowing the development of creative processes. In this case we can further illustrate this argument by focusing on each of the three elements influencing creativity: the social organization of the symbolic system; the symbolic system; and the individual (Csikszentmihalyi, 1996).

Redarding the social organization of the symbolic system, as we have seen, each discipline is regulated by gatekeepers, going from the family to people and institutions holding economic or intellectual power in that area. According to Csikszentmihalyi, this field of social forces can favor the creative production of individuals by means of seven factors: (1) by offering young people a good education; (2) by communicating to young people that a lot is expected from them; (3) by offering economical and cultural resources and allowing full access to knowledge; (4) by recognizing people's novel contributions at some point in their journey; (5) by allowing individuals to cultivate the hope of seeing one's own skills and efforts recognized; (6) by offering real opportunities to move and act within a discipline; and (7) by offering both intrinsic and extrinsic rewards (Csikszentmihalyi, 1996).

As we can see, all of these actions involve the fundamental factors, leading to the development of behavior, considered in this volume: increase of skills, presence of high challenges, balance between skills and challenges when both are high, intrinsic motivation, and self-determination.

Second, creativity is affected by the symbolic system. The characteristics of the different symbolic systems, such as painting, mathematics, medicine, or anthropology, can favor the development of creativity or not favor it. In particular, there seem to be two factors favoring creativity: the ease of accessing information, and the modalities and rules with which knowledge is stored and organized (Csikszentmihalyi, 1996).

Accessing information depends on the clarity of the language adopted and on the possibility for many to be able to know and use such language, whatever it might be. Organization of knowledge is a complex topic. On the one hand, it is easier to develop and recognize the creative product when the rules and criteria of the symbolic system are well defined and clear. This is the case, for instance, of a historical period in which esthetic criteria are common and shared, or in which (in a different domain) the rules of science are accepted as unambiguous and universals. On the other hand, a discipline is able to generate something new only when an internal instability and the psychic processes of an individual converge, enabling the resolution of such instability (Gardner, 1993; Csikszentmihalyi, 1996).

These two poles, clarity of rules and instability of the system, seem to represent two different challenges, both potentially productive for the development of the creative process. In fact, they constitute specific opportunities for those individuals having, respectively, the specific skills allowing them to introduce new information into an already regulated system, or specific skills allowing them to create a complex order in a momentarily unbalanced system. What these two types of individuals seem to have in common is, once more, the quality of subjective experience that they are able to derive when they express their respective creative styles. Such experiences are characterized by a balance of challenges and skills. The latter are, in both cases, qualitatively different but still in balance, and they therefore favor the development of an emergent and negentropic experience.

Third, the creative person must have specific and adequate traits and competencies, both biological and cognitive. In addition, one must act on these competencies in a specific way: by favoring a

117

duality that allows the individual, on the one hand, to be open and receptive, and on the other hand to be able to focus on goals and to work hard to achieve them, while following the rules of the system (Csikszentmihalyi, 1996). This duality represents a form of psychic complexity that reminds us of the previously mentioned "autotelic personality." In this case, too, we face the possibility of developing abilities that enable the individual to confront the rules of the external world. At the same time they enable the person to reformulate the demands and opportunities offered by the culture so that these come close to one's deepest motivations and allow for the experience to be positive, and for the production of new information. It seems evident that family, academic, or recreational contexts facilitating the development of this duality have a positive effect on the development of an individual's creativity.

To conclude, creativity represents a particular aspect of optimal experience. In fact, the creative process is based on an integrated relationship between, on the one hand, the individual's motivation and cognitive competencies (which can be defined as skills), and, on the other, the characteristics of the environmental demands, both symbolic and social, proposed by the external context (which can be defined as challenges). Furthermore, we shall repeat what we have already mentioned regarding the innovative elements of optimal subjective experience in general. The latter is characterized by the possibility of discovering emergent motivations and of addressing one's own behavior toward new and not predetermined social challenges. The centrality of optimal experience is also highlighted in a domain parallel to creativity, a domain concerned with the development of young talents (Csikszentmihalyi and Robinson, 1986).

In particular, we shall mention a longitudinal study, carried out by researchers at The University of Chicago, that analyzed the daily experience of more than 200 academically talented adolescents (Csikszentmihalyi, Rathunde and Whalen, 1993). The study began when students were in their freshman year of high school and ended their senior year. At the end of the study, the sample was divided between subjects who were still highly involved in the discipline in which they were particularly talented (and which they

intended to pursue academically) and subjects who did not cultivate their exceptional talent but were lead in a different direction.
The longitudinal analysis of the subjective experience of these two
samples (the data having been gathered by repetitive administra-
tions of the Experience Sampling Method, and by in-depth interviews) showed data that seem to confirm the importance of the
experience of flow. The first group of subjects is in fact characterized
by the tendency of having optimal experiences much more often
than the subjects of the second sample. This tendency is already present at the beginning of high school and it develops especially in situations related to the area in which the subjects are most talented.
The latter is the main discriminating factor. In the second sample,
states of anxiety and apathy are much more frequent.

In other words, the adolescents who were able to develop and
apply their talent in concrete social opportunities (in an academic
or working environment), and to offer innovative contributions,
are those who are able to have an optimal experience in dedicating
themselves to the discipline in which they are talented. On the
other hand, those who, although still highly competent, will not be
able to actually operationalize their skills, do not succeed in the
psychic strategy connecting talent, optimal experience, and the
areas in which they are talented.

In order to better understand these different outcomes it is useful to appeal once more to the concept of the autotelic personality.
It can be hypothesized that the subjects of the first group are characterized by a greater flexibility, are more able to tolerate frustra-
tion, boredom, and anxiety, and can reorganize their experience
even when facing demanding or overly normative challenges.
They therefore possess that specific set of metaskills that we have
defined as constituting the autotelic personality.

3.3 OPTIMAL EXPERIENCE AND CULTURAL CHANGE

In the first part of this volume we pointed out that the human
species is characterized by two concurrent processes of evolution

119

of information: biological and cultural. Cultural evolution is a historical and transgenerational process by which information deposited in extrasomatic sites (viz., externally with respect to the human body) is transmitted over time (Csikszentmihalyi, 1993; Massimini, Toscano and Inghilleri, 1993). Artifacts are the basic units of this evolving process: utensils, weapons, clothes, books, electronic devices, norms, technologies, social institutions, and all other kinds of human artificial products representing cultural vehicles and replicators.

We also pointed out that cultural information is not autonomously transmitted. Its tendency to increase in complexity and negentropy derives from the application of external forces proper to the living organism and, basically, from human beings' investment of psychic energy. In short, a law, an institution, a household object, and artifacts generally, are maintained and transmitted over time only insofar as individuals direct their attention toward them, select them, maintain them, and pass them on to other members of the population. The centrality of subjective experience for the processes of cultural transmission is therefore apparent.

Furthermore, the psychological sciences have already shown that a culture and its values are transmitted through socialization agencies, schools, and families in the first place, which allow the young members of the society to internalize the social rules. This internalization occurs in the actual daily life of people experiencing emotions, cognitions, and motivations, in connection with familial, academic, and social contexts (Csikszentmihalyi and Csikszentmihalyi Selega, 1988; Brislin, 1990; Segall, Dasen, Berry and Poortinga, 1990; Stigler, Shweder and Herdt, 1990; Berry, Poortinga, Segall and Dasen, 1992; Csikszentmihalyi, 1993; Lonner and Malpass, 1994; Triandis, 1994; Adler and Gielen, 1993; Wertsch, del Rio and Alvarez, 1995; Berry, Poortinga, Pandey, Dasen, Saraswathi, Segall and Kagitcibasi, 1996; Matsumoto, 1996; Simpson and Kenrick, 1996; Sue, Ivery and Pedersen, 1996; Suzuki, Meller and Ponterotto, 1996).

3.3.1 Transmission of Culture

The theories of self-determined and optimal subjective experience proposed in this volume (as related to concepts concerning the transmission of cultural information over time) allow us to describe synthetically, and, from a new perspective, the modalities according to which a culture is transmitted.

In the first place, a human culture is maintained and reproduced over time only insofar as it is able to attract individuals' psychic energy and to have them experience intrinsic motivation, self-determination, and optimal experience in connection with the specific elements of which it is composed. In this way there is a first coupling of the cultural teleonomic project and the psychological teleonomic project: Cultural structures and experiential structures are repeated over time in a harmonious fashion.

For instance, let us take into consideration the concept of challenge proposed by the theory of flow. Challenges represent a set of cultural rules that an individual has to face with his or her own skills. These rules, such as the norms concerning the relationship between parents and children in a Western family, have developed over time by means of the process of cultural evolution. If the individuals are internally motivated to adopt this type of family interaction, the regular repetition of the cultural norm and the regular repetition of the experiential state of intrinsic motivation, or flow, will simultaneously take place.

Furthermore, a human society can face the challenges offered by its relationship with other populations, both at the cultural and economic level, only insofar as it possesses not only efficient mechanisms able to transmit its own values, but it is also able to produce change and be flexible, in order to be able to sustain intercultural competition. Recent discussions of cultural evolution suggest a definition of harmonious bicultural selection. Studies on societies facing modernization have pointed out the advantage of modalities of social and normative organization that integrate the modernization (coming from the outside) and the older traditions proper to the specific population. A society that tends to cultivate exclusively traditional elements, or to the contrary a society that tends to abandon them solely to welcome more modern elements, are both at a disadvantage with respect to a culture that develops a more complex system of social instructions in which what is new and what is old are integrated in a harmonious and original fashion, thus producing an innovative sociocultural configuration (Inghilleri and Terranova-Cecchini, 1991; Delle Fave, Massimini and Maletto, 1991b).

This discussion therefore shows that processes of optimal cultural evolution are not only characterized by the regular transmission of information but are also characterized by the capacity to introduce new elements into the system. Furthermore, this fully tallies with the concepts of teleonomy and negentropy, characteristic of information presented in the first part of this volume: from this perspective, the theories here proposed seem to be particularly important. These in fact point out the evolving and emergent aspects of psychic functioning in addition to those concerning regularities. In this regard one might think of the concepts of emergent motivation, of optimal experience connected to the facing of new challenges, or of self-determined behavior proposed by Deci and Ryan. All of these theoretical elements point out the possibility for individuals to develop autonomous, and not predetermined, new experiences and behaviors. These innovations are the basis for cultural change.

The theory of optimal experience and the concept of autotelic personality have also shown an additional connection, within the context of this discussion, between cultural evolution and the quality of subjective experience. A family providing autotelic contexts is, in a certain sense, a bicultural family. This is to say that it is a family in which tradition, that which has been consolidated and is now known, is brought alongside the search for the novel and risky. The youngster is therefore able to experience in a positive way the integration between the different types of cultural information. In this way, a "short circuit" occurs between culture, its primary socialization agents, and subjective experience. As a consequence of this process the individual will tend to develop a complex personality and to search for and develop contexts for action – that is, cultural elements characterized by the same level of complexity.

We have here a very efficient mechanism of psychosocial dynamics that allows human groups to develop while simultaneously taking into consideration tradition, subjective well-being, and change. This mechanism further specifies the general integrative processes of known categories with innovations. These processes have been brought to light by the modern psychological literature and have found their formalization in established theories such as Moscovici's theory of social representations (Moscovici, 1981; 1984).

3.3.2 Subjective Experience and Rites of Passage

For several years numerous research groups have been gathering an enormous quantity of data regarding the relationship between individual psychic processes and cultural processes.[4]

One of the main points of these studies concerns, as we have said, the modalities according to which a society is able to direct youngsters' attention processes, motivations, and subjective experience toward meaningful goals connected with positive values in the culture. This is not a new topic within the social sciences: certain classical anthropological studies had already efficiently tackled these issues. For instance, consider the structure of the so-called rites of passage (Van Gennep, 1909). In most societies these rites accompany changes in the social status of an individual or group of individuals, while in other cases they accompany seasonal changes.

Van Gennep individuates three phases of a rite of passage: separation, liminality, and aggregation. In the first phase individuals are radically separated from their habitual situation: There is a change in space (e.g., the individual exits the village to enter the forest), time (the daily routine can be largely modified), and physical aspect (change in clothes, often almost complete nudity, the shaving of hair).

In the liminal phase, the subjects live in a sort of social limbo that belong neither to the preceding nor to the future condition: It is in this area that profound changes occur. In the third phase, aggregation, the individuals, by means of specific symbols and actions (as for instance new bodily decorations, new cloths, or ritual processions), fully reenter the customary daily life contexts (the family, social groups, the village). But these individuals are no longer the same as they were before. Their status is changed and their identity is also profoundly modified.

What is so meaningful in the rite of passage – in particular in the liminal phase – and what is its relationship with the theories presented here? In a peculiar space, which belongs neither to the past nor to the future, the subject in the rite of passage is urged by the elders, or by whoever holds tribal knowledge, to face new tasks and acquire new knowledge under a very specific normative condition (viz., well defined but not characteristic of the habitual social existence). The individual, protected by the presence of the elders and by the structure of the rite, approaches the risk of acquiring new skills which will allow him or her to fully achieve a new status and re-enter society.

This occurs in a liminal (Turner, 1982) and rather particular situation in which the historical memory of the population, derived from cultural evolution, can be rapidly and intensely deposited in the mind of youngsters. This internalization occurs thanks to specific experiences that can be superimposed on the ones proper to flow. This is to say that they are characterized by high concentration, a sense of self-determination (connected also to external rewards – i.e., the successful change in status – and therefore accompanied by the presence of integrated extrinsic motivation), and balance between the challenges offered at that moment and the available skills.

The rite of passage represents a prototype of the mechanisms of socialization that occur in a more differentiated and diluted way in contemporary societies. It can also be argued that the lack of social events comparable in a modern form to the rites of passage is one of the factors that today makes it difficult for many youngsters to undergo an integrated development. Therefore, young people tend to turn to other contexts, at times deviant, that allow them to change status, to have the sense of possessing higher skills, and to have a positive subjective experience.

3.3.3 Subjective Experience and Bicultural Evolution

The theories proposed in this volume can also contribute to a better understanding of the phenomena of human bicultural evolution. Included in this context are studies of specific populations that present bicultural development, such as the Navajo tribe, a Native-American population settled in the southwest of the United States (Massimini, Csikszentmihalyi and Delle Fave, 1988; Delle Fave, 1991; Inghilleri and Delle Fave, 1996). The bicultural organization that is basically found within this population expresses itself at various levels and is characterized by an integrated copresence of ancient cultural elements and modern elements.

On the one hand, we can observe the maintenance of complex forms of traditional tribal organization (e.g., clan division and the subsequent law of exogamous marriage) and the presence of an ancestral ceremonial system still alive and practiced today. The general conception of the world is still based on millenary values and rules, recorded in the tribe's myths and ceremonies. The lifestyle and the subsistence system of a seminomadic and pastoral type have also remained unchanged for generations in large portions of the Reserve (Kluckhohn and Leighton, 1946; Reichard, 1950; Inghilleri, 1988).

The close and often conflictual contact with the U.S. government and with American culture, the necessity to assert one's rights as far as the utilization of the territory is concerned, and the understanding that the development of the tribe is also based on secondary instruction of youngsters, have brought the acceptance of some factors characteristic of modern American society. It has not been a fully passive process, however, but an attempt to at least partially integrate the two cultural worlds. An example of this integration is a college (the Navajo Community College) that, along with teaching traditional subjects, such as the Navajo

125

language or local pharmacology based on herbs, also offers classes in modern academic disciplines. Another example is the possibility for youngsters to become acquainted with the original myths of the tribe by means of computers or videocassettes.

This bicultural system then manifests itself in specific social behaviors, such as the organization of traditional propitiatory ceremonies before facing demanding legal or political missions to the federal capital (Correll and Watson, 1972). Field research (Inghilleri and Delle Fave, 1996) pointed out that these social bicultural aspects are sustained by the possibility for young Navajos to have an integrated experience (internally motivated and flow-like) in a dual context, both modernized and traditional. In other words, the Navajo extended family and social institutions guarantee stimuli and reassurance, that is to say positive challenges and the perception of possessing adequate skills in situations tied both to ancient cultural factors (e.g., a curative ceremony or daily contact with the extended family) and to modern situations (e.g., the study of technical or more generally Western subjects).

It is therefore the positive quality of subjective experience that allows young Navajos to direct their attention alternately toward ancient and modern factors, thus realizing the transmission over time of the former and their original integration with the latter.

3.3.4 The Optimal Triad

The centrality of subjective experience for cultural evolution manifests itself in diverse contexts typical of Western contemporary society: adolescent American students (Csikszentmihalyi and Larson, 1984), Italian workers (Delle Fave and Massimini, 1988), American workers (Csikszentmihalyi and LeFevre, 1989), Chicago housewives (Wells, 1986), young Italian drug-addicts (Negri, Cesa-Bianchi and Delle Fave, 1992), and many other social domains (Csikszentmihalyi, 1993). The data show, in the different domains, the usefulness of the *optimal triad:* repetition of known rules, possibility for innovation, and sense of self-determination.

For instance, let us consider the working world, the world of corporations. It is well known that firms and work groups find

126

themselves in a positive situation when they are able simultaneously to express their own culture and rules with clarity and continuity, to develop autonomy and be innovative, and to allow team members to feel motivated, autonomous, and able to reconcile their skills with the tasks required from them.

The same process seems to be optimal in the educational and academic worlds. Advanced Italian experiences in the organization of kindergartens, as for instance in Reggio Emilia (Edwards, Gandini and Forman, 1993), try to favor autonomous choices and the development of children's specific competencies while remaining in a precise context of rules that allow children to express their own creativity and autonomy while being protected by the security offered by a known world, in both cognitive and affective terms. The practice – according to which every morning at least one of the parents takes the child to the kindergarten and for a certain period of time remains actively with him or her, with the other children and their parents, and with the teachers – is to be viewed in this light. This takes place in a central common area similar to the central square of many small Italian towns where people meet at the beginning of the day before going to work. Only after this first phase of social exchange will the child begin the various play and learning activities with peers and teachers. These activities focus on the development of self-determined choices within the domain of specific symbolic systems and within specific activities having their rules: numbers, music, drawing, the building of objects, bodily expression, and so on. The whole process seems to allow for a coupling of the external society (expressed by the square) with the symbolic systems and their rules, the family culture (the parents, present and active in the academic environment, are involved in and generally motivated by and pleased with this daily experience), and the children and their subjective experiences. The latter, day after day, bring about the development of the children's internal world and identities in connection with the culture to which they belong.

The optimal triad also seems to be active in politics. Consider, for instance, the government currently in place in Italy.[5] There is a coalition of parties ranging from the extreme left, to the ex-communist party, to the Catholic party, to moderate liberal forces close to the industrial world. This miracle of political engineering derives part of its strength from the ability to integrate norms, establishing a continuity with the past, with innovative norms. This is expressed in both the economic domain and in the domain of the choices of social politics (e.g., education or health).

Slowly a new generation is replacing the old ruling class, and several women are becoming responsible for governmental departments (even if only of a social nature like the Department of Health or the Italian "Ministero per la Famiglia" [tr.: Family Department]). One of the main expressed objectives of the government, in addition to economic growth, is to reestablish in youngsters trust in the country and to give them the chance of finding employment, which allows not only for survival and economic growth but also for the expression of one's own choices and skills. The "old" political categories of right and left are partly overridden. Therefore, a project taking into consideration, more or less consciously, the concepts of self-determination, intrinsic motivation, extrinsic motivation, and development of individual and social complexity, is most likely to attract the attention and the consensus of the citizens and hence to last over time.

3.3.5 Individual Differences and Social Communion

From a general point of view, and in particular for cross-cultural psychology (Inghilleri, 1994), such an approach is also significant in that it allows us to identify some constants and regularities in psychic processes, while respecting the diversity and the specificity of each individual and of each culture.

Self-determination and flow theories are in fact conceptions that focus their interest on the phenomenological aspects of experience and not on the contents of the experience itself. In other words, the theories limit themselves to defining an optimal modality of organization of the psychic apparatus, being characterized by an integrated and ordered relationship between the different components of the internal world and between internal world and external context.

These theories do not claim to define a priori the activities, situations, relationships, and rules (which is to say, the specific cultural contents of experience) able to bring about this positive state of consciousness. This is to say that individuals are able to develop their own autonomy and their own optimal experience in an original way, even within the domain of the cultural characteristics within which they formed their own identity and skills, and which continue to offer challenges in daily life. We therefore find the full expression of an individual's choices and motivations, which manifest themselves because of their connection with the values of the culture.

This concept comes close to the concept of "authenticity" expressed by Taylor (1992). This author points out that three sources of problems and discomfort are present in modernity: individualism, the primacy of "instrumental reason," and the narrowing of actual political freedom. These three problems are interconnected.

Let us follow Taylor's reasoning. Individualism is considered by many to be one of the major successes of modernity in that society allows individuals to choose their own values and lifestyles. But according to Taylor, this freedom is achieved at a cost: the loss of the old moral horizon derived from the fact that individuals saw themselves as part of a larger, cosmic, religious, and social order:

> the dark side of individualism is a centering on the self, which both flattens and narrows our lives, makes them poorer in meaning, and less concerned with others or society (Taylor, 1992, p.4).

This phenomenon is accompanied, in modernity, by instrumental reason, a type of rationality whose goal is maximum efficiency and the best cost–benefit ratio with respect to means and aims. The loss of the "sacred" in society determines that material aspects, the demands of pure economic growth, and the technology that develops further away from the individual, take over the real needs of the person. The consequence is the danger of seriously impoverishing our lives.

For Taylor, these two problems, individualism and instrumental reason, bear consequences at the political level. The institutions and structures of a technological–industrial society, based on these two factors, greatly constrain individual choices by not allowing for certain behaviors and by denying opportunities that are not material or have no economic value. Another kind of loss of freedom then occurs by means of a decreased involvement and desire to actively contribute to political institutions.

Taylor thoroughly discusses the first problem – individualism and loss of meaning. He proposes a path for change that he calls "the ethics of authenticity." To narcissism, hedonism, and permissiveness, Taylor opposes authenticity. On the one hand, for Taylor, authenticity and self-realization are based on a process according to which

> being true to myself means being true to my own originality, and that is something only I can articulate and discover. In articulating it, I am also defining myself. I am realizing a potentiality that is properly my own (*ibid.*, p.29).

On the other hand, authenticity presupposes that behind self-fulfillment and self-realization there has to be a moral force or idea. By this, Taylor understands

> a picture of what a better or higher mode of life would be, where "better" and "higher" are defined not in terms of what we happen to desire or need, but offer a standard of what we ought to desire (*ibid.*, p.16).

We have pointed out several times that the development of both individual and social complexity derive from an alliance between the individual's choices and motivations – also emergent motivations – and the rules of culture: In this case, there is a coupling of psychological and cultural teleonomy. This same alliance seems to be the basis of the concept of authenticity. In fact, Taylor claims that a sense of meaningful existence derives from two factors. The first is the perception that we are free to determine ourselves. This concept parallels those of intrinsic motivation, self-determination as expressed by Deci and Ryan, and autotelic activity.

A second factor must be simultaneously present, which is the

> understanding that *independent of my will* there is something noble, courageous, and hence significant in giving shape to my own life (*ibid.*, p.39).

In other words, the concept of authenticity presupposes that "the ideal of self-choice supposes that there are other issues of significance beyond self-choice" (*ibid.*, p.39). Self-determination is truly expressed only when it is automatically coupled with the values and rules of the culture and with the norms of the society – we could say: with cultural teleonomy.

This concept is reexamined and reiterated by Taylor when he claims once more that freedom and autonomy are today inseparably tied to the self, which is to say, the ideal of authenticity requires individuals to discover and articulate their identity. According to Taylor, this process has two aspects: one concerns the manner, the other the matter or the content of the process. The first one must necessarily be self-referential: authenticity must follow the individual's orientation and goals. But this does not mean that the other aspect, the content, must be self-referential; it can, instead, be tied to social values, norms, and aims: "I can find fulfillment in God, or a political cause, or tending the earth" (*ibid.*, p.82). Only in this way is true authenticity realized. In other words, I can and have to find optimal experience and my self-determination only through a coupling with the rules of the culture.

3.3.6 Future Risks

We shall now discuss a last point concerning the relationship between subjective experience and cultural evolution. The latter, in this century and especially in recent decades, has, on a global scale, increasingly emphasized the importance of material objects:

objects to own and consume, and objects conferring status and identity (Csikszentmihalyi and Rochberg-Halton, 1981; Douglas and Isherwood, 1979; Csikszentmihalyi, 1993).

This is certainly not a new factor. As we have already seen, the relationship between the investment of psychic energy and artifacts is at the very basis of the birth and development of human cultures. The novelty is given by the intensity and unidirectionality of this relationship. Some authors have seen a possible domination of economy and of the consequent transformation of human and social relationships into solely material or monetary relationships (Polanyi, 1944). This is when objects are not used to satisfy psychic and social needs (such as happiness, individual well-being, solidarity, and social coparticipation). Instead the objects (endowed of a precise cost and economic meaning) are able, in a certain sense, to use psychic processes and subjective experience in order to reproduce themselves over time.[6]

Within this context, a new element was introduced in the last few years that has made the problem more complicated. In complex Western societies a new set of needs and agencies has been introduced toward which one's own psychic energy can be directed: that is, immaterial agencies. Power[7] and economical wealth are today more and more connected with the possibility of controlling knowledge, information, communication, and social and leisure activities, which are all immaterial elements (Beaud, 1994). Here the very possibility of having access to situations allowing for optimal experience to occur tends to become an object of consumption and a commodity.

A sign of this process is given by the increasingly greater importance attributed to multinationals that produce, distribute, and regulate products or activities pertaining to leisure, show business, and communication. Consider the world of the media, the world of entertainment, the world of computers. We are faced with a new situation: It is as if part of one's internal motivations, desires, and a part of people's social exchanges related to psychological development and well-being are directed, or at any rate are regulated, by outside forces.

From a different perspective, the satisfaction of internal needs tends to become a rule and almost a prescription. The reading of certain books, the recreational use of computers, seeing works of art and going to museums, and contact with nature – all activities normally associated with internal rewards – are increasingly becoming social expectations, and are used as elements conferring status and external rewards. Access to such activities is also increasingly regulated and depends more and more on purchasing power. Creating an entrance ticket to an artistic city such as Venice, or multinationals organizing leisure activities around large structures and then selling such services, are some examples of this mechanism.

This situation, from a strictly psychological point of view, entails a risk. In fact, when access to contexts allowing for the satisfaction of intrinsic motivation tied to immaterial factors becomes regulated, and the emergence itself of optimal experience becomes something like a norm imposed by the external world and a need whose resolution requires a purchasing price, the dynamics between the pole of free choice and the pole of normativeness – which constitutes the fundamental moment for the integrated development of both individual and society – is interrupted.

From the point of view of the evolution of both the self and the culture to which one belongs, a situation is created that is far from emergent and self-generative conditions. As we have seen, the latter are the basis of developmental processes. We are facing the risk of an unchanged and almost inflexible replication of both internal and external cultural instructions. Such a phenomenon leads to a progressive disturbance of individual and social development.

To conclude, this last reflection brings us to emphasize the practical value of the theoretical views proposed in this volume. Two forces continuously run through the scenarios of daily life in which individuals, families, groups, and populations build their identities and organization: the maintenance of what is known, which derives from slow, demanding, and significant processes of historical accumulation of information on the one hand, and the autonomous development of novelties and original solutions satisfying the free choice of individuals and groups on the other. In this way it is possible to discern a path leading toward the integration of individual and social well-being, of intrinsic and extrinsic motivations, of social values and personal life themes, of common aims and individual objectives.

NOTES

CHAPTER 1. BASIC CONCEPTS

1. As we know, the gene is the fundamental unit of biological heredity. From a chemical point of view, it is constituted by the deoxyribonucleic acid, or DNA, which is the fundamental hereditary material of all organisms.

   In higher organisms, as for instance in human beings, the DNA is mainly located in the chromosomes of the cell's nucleus. The DNA codifies, in a sophisticated way, all the information that determines the different structures of an organism. This information is also transmitted by means of specific reproductive mechanisms from the mother-cells to the daughter-cells, and by means of the gametes, or sexual cells, from one individual to another in the following generation.

2. The reader will find the word *integrated* several times in the text. This term is to be understood as meaning "complex and ordered." More specifically, by *integrated experience* we mean a differentiated and complex experiential state primarily deriving from two elements: first, from the various psychic functions (motivation, cognition, volition, and emotion) working in an optimal, ordered, and connected fashion among themselves; secondly, from the needs and aims of the internal world being connected and in balance with the requirements of the external world. Authors such as Deci and Ryan use the term *integrated* in the same way: see for instance the concept of *integrated extrinsic motivation* mentioned later in the chapter (Deci and Ryan, 1985).

CHAPTER 2. THEORIES OF SUBJECTIVE EXPERIENCE AND THE DEVELOPMENT OF PERSONALITY

1. Two clarifications: first of all, it should be noted that when we speak of activity, the term is to be conceived broadly. In fact, flow can occur also in the absence of motor acts, as in the case of reading, thinking, meditating, contemplating, and daydreaming.

   Second, the term *autotelic* (from the Greek *autós* = oneself, and télos = aim) is introduced by Csikszentmihalyi (1975) in order to

135

define activities and experiences perceived as not having any other aim besides their taking place. These activities are done for their own sake (meaning they are not instrumental), as in the case of intrinsic motivation, considered earlier.

2. From a statistical point of view, the data are taken from the subjects' self-description of perceived challenges and skills. The latter, having been derived from specific scales, are then transformed into standard scores (Z-scores). The interaction of the two Cartesian axes corresponds to the "0" in both scales (for a description of the statistical model employed, see Carli, 1986; Massimini, Csikszentmihalyi and Carli, 1987; Massimini and Carli, 1988).

CHAPTER 3. SUBJECTIVE EXPERIENCE
AND SOCIAL CONTEXTS

1. The Italian term is *dereticolizzazione,* literally, "falling out of the network" or "out of the loop." It has therefore stronger connotations than the closest English term, *marginalization.* Its theoretical importance should be understood with reference to a theory in which healthy individuals cannot be understood outside the context of their cultural networks. [Translator's note]
2. In addition to these three general approaches, we should mention the original methodology of sociological and historiographical research proposed by Simonton (1984a, 1984b).
3. Among the cognitive approaches, we shall also mention Gruber's valuable studies (Gruber, 1982; Gruber and Davis, 1988) and Feldman's research (1980, 1988). And the latter proposes a highly interactive approach.
4. See the authors mentioned at the beginning of this chapter.
5. Summer 1998.
6. It should be noted that here also we come close, at least partially, to Taylor's thought, in particular to the concept of instrumental reason.
7. The definition of *power* is here to be understood both in its common sense and its social psychological sense: we shall define social power as "the potential influence of some influencing agent, O, over some person, P. Influence is defined as a change in cognition, attitude, behavior, or emotion of P which can be attributed to O." (Collins and Raven, 1969, p.160).

BIBLIOGRAPHY

Abelson, R. P. (1976). Script processing in attitude formation and decision making. In J. Carrol and J. Payne (Eds.), *Cognition and social behavior.* Hillsdale: Erlbaum.

Adler, L. L., and Gielen, U. P. (Eds.) (1993). *Cross-cultural topics in psychology.* New York: Praeger.

Ainsworth, M. D. S., Bell, S. M., and Stayton, D. J. (1971). Individual differences in strange-situation behavior of one-year-olds. In H. R. Schaffer (Ed.), *The origins of human social relations.* London: Academic Press.

Allport, G. W. (1961). *Pattern and growth in personality.* New York: Holt, Rinehart & Winston.

Amabile, T. M. (1983). *The social psychology of creativity.* New York: Springer-Verlag.

Amerio, P. (1982). *Teorie in psicologia sociale.* Bologna: Il Mulino.

Angyal, A. (1965). *Neurosis and treatment: A holistic theory.* New York: John Wiley.

Apter, M. J. (1989). *Reversal theory: Motivation, emotion and personality.* London: Routledge.

Arieti, S. (1976). *Creativity: The magic synthesis.* New York: Basic Books.

Baer, D. M. (1987). Do we really want the unification of psychology? *New Ideas in Psychology 5*, 355–60.

Bagnara, S. (1984). *L'Attenzione.* Bologna: Il Mulino.

Bakan, D. (1987). Psychology's digressions. *New Ideas in Psychology 5*, 347–50.

Bandura, A. (1977). *Social learning theory.* Englewood Cliffs: Prentice-Hall.

Barash, D. P. (1977). *Sociobiology and behavior.* New York: Elsevier.

Barkow, J. H. (1991). Precis of "Darwin, sex and status": Biological approaches to mind and culture. *Behavioral and Brain Sciences 14*, 295–334.

Barkow, J. H., Cosmides, S. L., and Tooby, J. (Eds.) (1992). *The adapted mind: Evolutionary psychology and the generation of culture.* New York: Oxford University Press.

Baumrind, D. (1989). Rearing competent children. In W. Damon (Ed.) *Child development today and tomorrow.* San Francisco: Jossey-Bass.

Beaud, M. (1994). Il Mondo si ribalta. *Le Monde Diplomatique* (It. Ed.), 1(6), 14–15.

Berlyne, D. E. (1960). *Conflict, arousal and curiosity.* New York: McGraw-Hill.

———. (1966). Exploration and curiosity. *Science 153*, 25–33.

———. (1978). Curiosity and learning. *Motivation and Emotion 2*, 97–175.

Berry, J. W., Poortinga, Y. H., Segall, M. H., and Dasen, P. R. (1992). *Cross-cultural psychology: Research and applications.* Cambridge, MA: Cambridge University Press.

Berry, J., Poortinga, Y., Pandey, J., Dasen, P., Saraswathi, S., Segall, M., and Kagitcibasi, C. (Eds.) (1996). *Handbook of cross-cultural psychology* (2nd ed.). Boston: Allyn and Bacon.

Boggiano, A. K., Shield, A., Barrett, M., Kellam, T., Thompson, E., Simons, J., and Katz, P. (1992). Helplessness deficits in students: The role of motivational orientation. *Motivation and Emotion 16*(3), 271–99.

Bowlby, J. (1969). *Attachment and loss: Vol. I, Attachment.* London: Hogarth Press.

Brislin, R. (1990). *Applied cross-cultural psychology.* Newbury Park, CA: Sage.

Broadbent, D. E. (1958). *Perception and communication.* London: Pergamon Press.

Burridge, K. (1979). *Someone, no one. An essay on individuality.* Princeton: Princeton University Press.

Calegari, P. (1992). *Osservatori della crisi.* Napoli: Liguori.

Carli, M. (1986). Selezione psicologica e qualità dell'esperienza. In F. Massimini and P. Inghilleri (Eds.), *L'Esperienza quotidiana. Teoria e metodo di analisi.* Milano: F. Angeli.

Carrithers, M., Collins, S., and Lukes, S. (Eds.) (1985). *The category of the person: Anthropology, philosophy and history.* Cambridge, MA: Cambridge University Press.

Cesa-Bianchi, M. (1987). *Psicologia dell'invecchiamento: Caratteristiche e problemi.* Roma: Nis.

Cherry, E. C. (1953). Some experiments on the recognition of speech, with one and with two ears. *Journal of the Acoustical Society of America 25*, 975–79.

Cloack, F. T. (1975). Is a cultural ethology possible? *Human Ecology 3*(3), 161–82.

Collins, B. E., and Raven, B. H. (1969). Group structure: Attraction, coalitions, communications and power. In G. Lindzey and E. Aronson (Eds.), *The handbook of social psychology* (Vol. 4), Reading, MA: Addison-Wesley.

Condry, J., and Stokker, L. G. (1992). Overview of special issue on intrinsic motivation. *Motivation and emotion 16*(3), 157–64.

Correll, J. L., Watson, E. L. (1972). *Welcome to the land of the Navajo. A book of information about the Navajo Indians.* Museum and Research Department the Navajo Tribe. Window Rock, Arizona.

Csikszentmihalyi, M. (1975). *Beyond boredom and anxiety.* San Francisco: Jossey-Bass.

———. (1978a). Attention and the holistic approach to behavior. In K. S. Pope and J. L. Singer (Eds.), *The stream of consciousness.* New York: Plenum.

———. (1978b). Intrinsic reward and emergent motivation. In M.R. Lepper and D. Greene (Eds.), *The hidden costs of reward.* New York: Erlbaum.

———. (1981). Intrinsic motivation and effective teaching. In J. Bess (Ed.), *The motivation to teach.* San Francisco: Jossey-Bass.

———. (1982). Towards a psychology of optimal experience. In L. Wheeler (Ed.), *Review of personality and social psychology* (Vol. 2). Beverly Hills: Sage.

———. (1985). Emergent motivation and the evolution of the self. In D. Kleiber and M. H. Maehr (Eds.), *Motivation in adulthood.* Greenwich, CT: Jai Press.

———. (1986). Lo Studio dell'esperienza quotidiana. In F. Massimini and P. Inghilleri (Eds.), *L'esperienza quotidiana. Teoria e metodo di analisi.* Milano: F. Angeli.

———. (1988a). Society, culture and person: A system view of creativity. In R. J. Sternberg (Ed.), *The nature of creativity.* Cambridge, MA: Cambridge University Press.

———. (1988b). The flow experience and its significance for human psychology. In M. Csikszentmihalyi and I. Csikszentmihalyi Selega (Eds.), *Optimal experience. Studies of flow in consciousness.* Cambridge, MA: Cambridge University Press.

———. (1990). *Flow. The psychology of optimal experience.* New York: Harper-Collins.

———. (1993). *The evolving self. A psychology for the third millenium.* New York: Harper-Collins.

———. (1996). *Creativity. Flow and the psychology of discovery and invention.* New York: Harper-Collins.

———. (1997). *Finding flow. The psychology of engagement with everyday life.* New York: Harper-Collins.

Csikszentmihalyi, M., and Csikszentmihalyi Selega, I. (Eds.) (1988). *Optimal experience: Studies of flow in consciousness.* Cambridge, MA: Cambridge University Press.

Csikszentmihalyi, M., and Figurski, T. (1982). Self-awareness and aversive experience in everyday life. *Journal of Personality 50,* 15–28.

Csikszentmihalyi, M., and Graef, R. (1980). The experience of freedom in daily life. *American Journal of Community Psychology 8,* 401–414.

Csikszentmihalyi, M., and Kubey, R. (1981). Television and the rest of life. *Public Opinion Quarterly 45,* 317–28.

Csikszentmihalyi, M., and Larson, R. (1978). Intrinsic rewards in school crime. *Crime and delinquency 24,* 322–35.

———. (1984). *Being adolescent: Conflict and growth in the teenage years.* New York: Basic Books.

———. (1987). Validity and reliability of the experience sampling method. *The Journal of Nervous and Mental Disease 175*(9), 525–36.

Csikszentmihalyi, M., Larson, R., and Prescott, S. (1977). The ecology of adolescent activity and experience. *Journal of Youth and Adolescence 6,* 281–94.

Csikszentmihalyi, M., and LeFevre, J. (1989). Optimal experience in work and leisure. *Journal of Personality and Social Psychology 56,* 815–22.

Csikszentmihalyi, M., and Massimini, F. (1985). On the psychological selection of bio-cultural information. *New Ideas in Psychology 3*(2), 115–38.

Csikszentmihalyi, M., and Nakamura, J. (1989). The dynamics of intrinsic motivation: A study of adolescents. In *Research on motivation in education,* vol. 3, *Goals and cognitions.* New York: Academic Press.

Csikszentmihalyi, M., and Rathunde, K. (1993). The measurement of flow in everyday life: Toward a theory of emergent motivation. In *Nebraska symposium on motivation* (Vol. 40). Lincoln: University of Nebraska Press.

———. (1998). The development of the person: An experiential perspective on the ontogenesis of psychological complexity. In W. Damon and R. M. Lerner (Eds.), *Handbook of child psychology.* New York: John Wiley.

Csikszentmihalyi, M., Rathunde, K., and Whalen, S. (1993). *Talented teenagers: A longitudinal study of their development.* Cambridge, MA: Cambridge University Press.

Csikszentmihalyi, M., and Robinson, R. (1986). Culture, time, and the development of talent. In R. J. Sternberg and J. E. Davidson (Eds.), *Conceptions of giftedness.* New York: Cambridge University Press.

Csikszentmihalyi, M., and Rochberg-Halton, E. (1981). *The meaning of things.* Cambridge, MA: Cambridge University Press.

Darwin, C. (1859). *On the origin of species by means of natural selection.* London: Murray.

Davinson, D., and Davinson, R. (Eds.) (1980). *The psychobiology of consciousness.* Plenum, New York.

Davison, G. C., and Neale, J. M. (1986). *Abnormal psychology. An experimental clinical approach.* New York: John Wiley.

Dawkins, R. (1976). *The selfish gene.* New York: Oxford University Press.

―――. (1982). *The extended phenotype.* Oxford: W. H. Freeman & Co.

Dazi, N. (Ed.). (1981). *James. Antologia di scritti psicologici.* Bologna: Il Mulino.

DeCharms, R. (1968). *Personal causation: The internal affective determinants of behavior.* New York: Academic Press.

Deci, E. L. (1971). Effects of externally mediated rewards on intrinsic motivation. *Journal of Personality and Social Psychology 18,* 105–115.

―――. (1972). Intrinsic motivation, extrinsic reinforcement and inequity. *Journal of Personality and Social Psychology 92,* 113–20.

―――. (1975). *Intrinsic motivation.* New York: Plenum.

―――. (1980). *The psychology of self-determination.* Lexington: Lexington Books.

Deci, E. L., Connell, J. P., and Ryan, R. M. (1989). Self-determination in a world organization. *Journal of Applied Psychology 74,* 580–90.

Deci, E. L., and Ryan, R. M. (1980). The empirical exploration of intrinsic motivational processes. In L. Berkovitz (Ed.), *Advances in experimental social psychology* (Vol. 13). New York: Academic Press.

―――. (1985). *Intrinsic motivation and self-determination in human behavior.* New York: Plenum.

―――. (1991). A motivational approach to self: Integration in personality. In R. Dienstbier (Ed.), *Nebraska symposium on motivation* (Vol. 38). *Perspectives on Motivation.* Lincoln: University of Nebraska Press.

Delle Fave, A. (1991). Esperienza ottimale e processi di modernizzazione: La strategia bi-culturale dei Navajo. In P. Inghilleri and R. Terranova-Cecchini (Eds.), *Avanzamenti in psicologia transculturale.* Milano: F. Angeli.

Delle Fave, A., and Larson, R. 1993. Solitudine ed evoluzione culturale. In F. Massimini and P. Inghilleri (Eds.), *La selezione psicologica umana. Teoria e metodo di analisi.* Milano: Cooperativa Libraria Iulm.

Delle Fave, A., and Massimini, F. (1988). Modernization and the changing contexts of flow in work and leisure. In M. Csikszentmihalyi, I. Csikszentmihalyi Selega (Eds.), *Optimal experience. Psychological studies of flow in consciousness.* Cambridge, MA: Cambridge University Press.

―――. (1992). Experience sampling method and the measuring of clinical change: A case of anxiety disorder. In M. W. DeVries (Ed.), *The experience of psychopathology. Investigating mental disorders in their natural settings.* Cambridge, MA: Cambridge University Press.

141

Delle Fave, A., Massimini, F., and Maletto, C. (1991a). Barboni. *Psicologia contemporanea 104*(marzo-aprile), 55–63.

———. (1991b). Processi di modernizzazione e selezione bi-culturale umana. In P. Inghilleri and R. Terranova-Cecchini (Eds.), *Avanzamenti in psicologia transculturale*. Milano: F. Angeli.

Denzin, N. K., and Lincoln, Y. S. (1994). *Handbook of qualitative research*. New York: Sage.

DeVries, M. W. (Ed.) (1992). *The experience of psychopathology. Investigating mental disorders in their natural settings*. Cambridge, MA: Cambridge University Press.

Douglas, M., and Isherwood, B. (1979). *The world of goods*. New York: Basic Books.

Durkheim, E. (1895). *Les Règles de la Méthode Sociologique*. Paris: Alcan.

Eccles, J. C. (1973). *The understanding of the brain*. New York: McGraw-Hill Book Company.

Edwards, C. P., Gandini, L., and Forman, G. E. (Eds.) (1993). *The hundred languages of children: The Reggio-Emilia approach to early childhood education*. Ablex, NJ: Norwood.

Ekman, P. (1972). Universal and cultural differences in facial expressions of emotions. In *Nebraska symposium on motivation* (Vol. 19), *Current theory in research on motivation*. Lincoln: Nebraska University Press.

Feldman, D. H. (1980). *Beyond universals in cognitive development*. Norwood, NJ: Ablex.

———. (1988). Creativity: Dreams, insights, and tranformations. In R. J. Sternberg (Ed.), *The nature of creativity*. Cambridge University Press, New York.

Feldman, M. W., and Cavalli-Sforza, L. L. (1978). Fenotipi, genotipi ed evoluzione culturale. In M. Poli (Ed.), *Genetica e psicologia*. Milano: F. Angeli.

Feldman, S. (1986). *Nature's gambit*. New York: Basic Books.

Festinger, L. (1957). *A theory of cognitive dissonance*. Stanford: Stanford University Press.

Field, T. (1985). Attachment as psychobiological attunement: Being on the same wavelength. In M. Reite and T. Field (Eds.), *The psychobiology of attachment and separation*. New York: Academic Press.

Fiske, D. W., and Maddi, S. R. (1961). *Functions of varied experience*. Homewood: Dorsey Press.

Fodor, J. K. (1983). *The modularity of mind*. Cambridge, MA: The MIT Press.

Freud, S. (1900). L'interpretazione dei sogni. In *Opere di Sigmund Freud (OSF)*, (Vol. 3), Bollati Boringhieri, Torino 1966.

142

————. (1910). Un ricordo d'infanzia di Leonardo da Vinci. *OSF* (Vol. 6), 1974.

————. (1916). Introduzione alla psicoanalisi. *OSF* (Vol. 8), 1976.

————. (1920). Al di là del principio del piacere. *OSF* (Vol. 9), 1977.

————. (1922). L'Io e l' Es. *OSF* (Vol. 9), 1977.

————. (1932). Introduzione alla psicoanalisi. Nuova serie di lezioni. *OSF* (Vol. 11), 1979.

Gardner, H. (1983). *Frames of mind.* New York: Basic Books.

————. (1988a). Creative lives and creative works: A synthetic scientific approach. In J. R. Sternberg (Ed.), *The nature of creativity.* Cambridge, MA: Cambridge University Press.

————. (1988b). Creativity: An interdisciplinary perspective. *Creativity Research Journal 1*(December), 8–26.

————. (1992). Scientific psychology. Should we bury it or praise it? *New Ideas in Psychology 10*, 179–90.

————. (1993). *Creating minds. An anatomy of creativity seen through the lives of Freud, Einstein, Picasso, Stravinsky, Eliot, Graham and Gandhi.* New York: Basic Books.

Gardner, H., and Wolf, C. 1988. The fruits of asynchrony from a psychological point of view. *Adolescent Psychiatry 15*, 106–123.

Grolnick, W. S., and Ryan, R. M. (1989). Parent styles associated with children's self-regulation and competence in school. *Journal of Educational Psychology 81*, 143–54.

Grotevant, H. D., and Cooper, C. R. (Eds.) (1983). *Adolescent development in the family.* San Francisco: Jossey-Bass.

Gruber, H. E. (1982). *Darwin on man.* Chicago: University of Chicago Press.

Gruber, H. E., and Davis, S. N. (1988). Inching our way up Mount Olympus: The evolving systems approach to creative thinking. In R. J. Sternberg (Ed.), *The nature of creativity.* New York: Cambridge University Press.

Hamilton, J. A. (1981). Attention, personality and the self-regulation of mood: Absorbing interest and boredom. In B. A. Maher (Ed.), *Progress in experimental personality research.* New York: Academic Press.

Hamilton, J. A., Haier, R. J., and Buchsbaum, M. S. (1984). Intrinsic enjoyment and boredom coping scales: Validation with personality, evoked potential and attention measures. *Personality and Individual Differences 5*(2), 183–93.

Harackiewicz, J. (1979). The effects of reward contingency and performance feedback on intrinsic motivation. *Journal of Personality and Social Psychology 37*, 1352–63.

Harlow, H. F. (1953). Motivation as a factor in the acquisition of new responses. In *Current theory and research on motivation*. Lincoln: University of Nebraska Press.

Harré, R., Lamb, R., and Mecacci, L. (1986). *The encyclopedic dictionary of psychology*. London: Basil Blackwell.

Harter, S., and Jackson, B. K. (1992). Trait vs. nontrait conceptualizations of intrinsic/extrinsic motivational orientation. *Motivation and Emotion* 16(3), 209–230.

Hartmann, H. (1958). *Ego psychology and the problem of adaptation*. New York: International Universities Press.

Heider, F. (1958). *The psychology of interpersonal relations*. New York: John Wiley.

Hektner, J. M. (1996). *Exploring optimal personality development: A longitudinal study of adolescents*. Unpublished dissertation. The University of Chicago, Committee on Human Development.

Heyman, G. D., and Dweck, C. S. (1992). Achievement goals and intrinsic motivation: Their relation and their role in adaptive motivation. *Motivation and Emotion* 16(3), 231–48.

Hilgard, E. (1980). The trilogy of mind: Cognition, affection and conation. *Journal of the History of the Behavioral Sciences 16*, 107–117.

Hoffman, J. E., Nelson, B., and Houck, M. R. (1983). The role of attentional resources in automatic detection. *Cognitive Psychology 51*, 379–410.

Huang, M. P. L. (1997). *Family context and social development in adolescence*. Unpublished dissertation. The University of Chicago, Committee on Human Development.

Hull, C. L. (1943). *Principles of behavior*. New York: Appleton.

Hunt, J . (1965). Intrinsic motivation and its role in psychological development. In D. Levine (Ed.), *Nebraska symposium on motivation* (Vol. 13). Lincoln: Nebraska University Press.

Hurlburt, R. T. (1990). *Sampling normal and schizophrenic inner experience*. New York: Plenum Press.

Inghilleri, P. (1986). Riflessioni teoretiche sulla pratica psichiatrica in Nicaragua. L'esperienza di Ciudad Sandino. In R. Terranova-Cecchini and L. Panzeri (Eds.), *Cooperazione in Nicaragua. La salute mentale. Teoria e pratica di psichiatria transculturale per lo sviluppo*. Milano: Grt.

———. (1988). Interazione tra approccio biologico e approccio psicologico in medicina: Uno studio transculturale. In M. Cesa-Bianchi and G. Sala (Eds.), *Umanità e scienza in medicina*. Milano: F. Angeli.

———. (1993a). La teoria del flusso di coscienza: Esperienza ottimale e sviluppo del sé. In F. Massimini and P. Inghilleri (Eds.), *La selezione psicologica umana. Teoria e metodo di analisi.* Milano: Cooperativa Libraria Iulm.

———. (1993b). Selezione psicologica bi-culturale: Verso l'aumento della complessità individuale e sociale. Il caso dei Navajo. In F. Massimini and P. Inghilleri (Eds.), *La selezione psicologica umana. Teoria e metodo di analisi.* Milano: Cooperativa Libraria Iulm.

———. (1994). Il contributo della psicologia transculturale alle scienze del comportamento. In J. W. Berry, Y. H. Poortinga, M. H. Segall and P. R. Dasen *Psicologia transculturale. Teoria, ricerca e applicazioni.* Milano: Guerini.

———. (1997). A new perspective on self-development: From the subjective experience to the psychosocial action. ICP regional conference. *Crosscultural perspectives on human development.* Padua, Abstracts, p.28.

Inghilleri, P., and Delle Fave, A. (1996). Competizione di flow: La selezione biculturale dei Navajo. In F. Massimini, P. Inghilleri and A. Delle Fave (Ed.), *La selezione psicologica umana. Teoria e metodo di analisi* (2nd ed.). Milano: Cooperativa Libraria Iulm.

Inghilleri, P., and Terranova-Cecchini, R. (Eds.) (1991). *Avanzamenti in psicologia transculturale* Milano: F. Angeli.

Isabella, R. A., and Belsky, J. (1991). Interactional synchrony and the origins of infant–mother attachment: A replication study. *Child Development 62,* 373–84.

Izard, C. E. (1977). *Human emotions.* New York: Plenum.

Izard, C. E., Kagan, J., and Zajonc, R. B. (1984). *Emotions, cognitions and behavior.* New York: Cambridge University Press.

James, W. (1890). *The principles of psychology.* (Vols. 1 and 2). New York: Dover Publications Inc.

Jung, C. G. (1928). *L'Io e l'inconscio.* Torino: Bollati Boringhieri, 1967.

———. (1939). *Coscienza, inconscio e individuazione.* Torino: Bollati Boringhieri, 1985.

Jodelet, D. (1984). Représentations sociales. Phénomènes, concept et théorie. In S. Moscovici (Ed.), *Psychologie sociale.* Paris: Puf.

Kahneman, D. (1973). *Attention and effort.* Englewood Cliffs: Prentice-Hall.

Keele, S. W. (1973). *Attention and human performance.* Pacific Palisades: Goodyear Publishing Co.

Kluckhohn, C., and Leighton, D. (1946). *The Navajo.* Cambridge, MA: Harvard University Press.

Krahé, B. (1992). *Personality and social psychology.* Newbury Park: Sage.

Krantz, D. L. (1987). Psychology's search for unity. *New Ideas in Psychology 5,* 329–39.

Kris, E. (1952). *Psychoanalytic explorations in art.* New York: International Universities Press.

Kruglansky, A. W. (1975). The endogenous–exogenous partition in attribution theory. *Psychological Review 82,* 387–406.

Kruglansky, A. W., Freedman, I., and Zeevi, G. (1971). The effects of extrinsic incentives on some qualitative aspects of task performance. *Journal of Personality 39,* 606–617.

Laing, R. D., and Esterson, A. (1964). *Sanity, madness and the family.* (Vol. I), *Families of schizophrenics.* London: Tavistock Publications.

Laplanche, J., and Pontalis, J. B. (1968). *The language of psychoanalysis.* New York: Norton.

Larson, R., and Csikszentmihalyi, M. (1983). The experience sampling method. In H. Reis (Ed.), *New directions for naturalistic methods in behavioral sciences.* San Francisco: Jossey-Bass.

Lepper, M. R., and Cordova, D. I. (1992). A desire to be taught: Instructional consequences of intrinsic motivation. *Motivation and Emotion 16*(3), 187–208.

Lepper, M. R., and Greene, D. (Eds.), (1978). *The hidden costs of reward.* Hillsdale: Erlbaum.

Lepper, M. R., Greene, D., and Nisbett, R. E. (1973). Undermining children's intrinsic interest with extrinsic rewards: A test of the "overjustification" hypothesis. *Journal of Personality and Social Psychology 28,* 129–37.

Lonner, W. J., and Malpass, R. R. (Eds.) (1994). *Psychology and culture.* Boston: Allyn & Bacon.

Lumsden, C. J., and Wilson, E. O. (1981). *Genes, mind, culture: The coevolutionary process.* Cambridge, MA: Harvard University Press.

Lutte, G. (1987). *Psicologia degli adolescenti e dei giovani.* Bologna: Il Mulino.

Marsella, A. J., De Vos, G., and Hsu, F. L. K. (Eds.) (1985). *Culture and self: Asian and Western perspectives.* London: Tavistock Publications.

Maslow, A. H. (1954). *Motivation and personality.* New York: Harper.

———. (1959). Cognition of being in the peak experience. *Journal of Genetic Psychology 94,* 43–66.

———. (1968). *Toward a psychology of being.* New York: Van Nostrand.

Massimini, F. (1993). I presupposti teorici del paradigma della selezione culturale umana. In F. Massimini, F., and P. Inghilleri (Eds.), *La selezione psicologica umana. Teoria e metodo di analisi.* Milano: Cooperativa Libraria Iulm.

Massimini, F., and Calegari, P. (1979). *Il contesto normativo sociale.* Milano: F. Angeli.

146

Massimini, F., and Carli, M. (1988). The systematic assessment of flow in daily experience. In M. Csikszentmihalyi and I. Csikszentmihalyi Selega (Eds.), *Optimal experience. Studies of flow in consciousness.* Cambridge, MA: Cambridge University Press.

Massimini, F., Csikszentmihalyi, M., and Carli, M. (1987). The monitoring of optimal experience. A tool for psychiatric rehabilitation. *Journal of Nervous and Mental Disease 175*(9), 545–49.

Massimini, F., Csikszentmihalyi, M., and Delle Fave, A. (1988). Flow and biocultural evolution. In M. Csikszentmihalyi and I. Csikszentmihalyi Selega (Eds.), *Optimal experience. Studies of flow in consciousness.* Cambridge, MA: Cambridge University Press.

Massimini, F., and Delle Fave, A. (1988). Variazioni della qualità dell'esperienza nella vita quotidiana: Proposte per la riabilitazione psichiatrica. In G. Ferrari, L. Masina and A. Merini (Eds.), *La riabilitazione del malato mentale: Problemi teorici ed esperienze cliniche.* Bologna: Clueb.

Massimini, F., and Inghilleri, P. (1986). *L'esperienza quotidiana. Teoria e metodo di analisi.* Milano: F. Angeli.

Massimini, F., and Inghilleri, P. (1993). *La selezione psicologica umana. Teoria e metodo di analisi.* Milano: Cooperativa Libraria Iulm.

Massimini, F., Inghilleri, P., and Delle Fave, A. (1996). *La selezione psicologica umana. Teoria e metodo di analisi*, seconda edizione. Milano: Cooperativa Libraria Iulm.

Massimini, F., Terranova-Cecchini, R., and Inghilleri, P. (1985). Cultural model and rehabilitation plan for varied forms of psychopatology. *Analytic Psychotherapy and Psychopathology 2*, 55–69.

Massimini, F., Toscano, M., and Inghilleri, P. (1993). La selezione culturale umana. In Massimini, F. and Inghilleri, P. (1993). *La selezione psicologica umana. Teoria e metodo di analisi.* Milano: Cooperativa Libraria Iulm.

Matsumoto, D. (1996). *Culture and psychology.* Pacific Grove, CA: Brooks/Cole.

Maturana, H., and Varela, F. (1980). *Autopoiesi and cognition. The realization of living.* Dordrecht: Reidel.

McClelland, D. C., Atkinson, J. W., Clarck, R. W., and Lowell, E. L. (1953). *The achievement motive.* New York: Appleton.

Mead, G. H. (1934). *Mind, self and society.* Chicago: University of Chicago Press.

Mecacci, L. (1994). *Storia della psicologia del Novecento.* Bari: Laterza.

Miller, G. A. (1956). The magical number seven, plus or minus two. Some limits on our capacity for processing information. *Psychological Review 63*, 81–97.

Miller, G. A., Galanter, E. M., and Pribram, K. H. (1960). *Plans and structure of behavior*. New York: Holt, Rinehart & Winston.

Miller, J. G. (1970). *Living systems*. New York: McGraw-Hill.

———. (1988). Bridging the content–structure dichotomy: Culture and the self. In M. H. Bond (Ed.), *The cross-cultural challenge to social psychology*. Newbury Park: Sage.

Monod, J. (1971). *Chance and necessity*. New York: Alfred A. Knopf.

Montgomery, K. C. (1954). The role of exploratory drive in learning. *Journal of Comparative and Physiological Psychology 47*, 360–64.

Morin, E. 1985. La via della complessità. In G. Bocchi and M. Ceruti (Eds.), *La sfida della complessità*. Milano: Feltrinelli.

Moscovici, S. (1961–76). *La psychanalyse: Son image et son public*. Paris: Puf.

———. (1973). Foreword. In Claudine Herzlich: *Health and illness: A social psychological analysis*. London & New York: Academic Press.

———. (1981). On social representations. In J. P. Forgas (Ed.), *Social cognition: Perspectives on everyday understanding*. London: Academic Press.

———. (1984). The phenomenon of social representations. In R. Farr and S. Moscovici (Eds.), *Social representations*. Cambridge, MA: Cambridge University Press.

Nathan, T. (1986). *La folie des autres. Traité d'ethnopsychiatrie clinique*. Paris: Dunod.

Negri, P., Cesa-Bianchi G., and Delle Fave, A. (1992). *Ristrutturazione dei processi di attenzione nei tossicodipendenti: Íl ruolo delle comunità*. Report dell'Istituto di Psicologia della Facoltà Medica, Università degli Studi di Milano, Novembre.

Neisser, U. (1967). *Cognitive psychology*. New York: Appleton-Century-Crofts.

Neisser, U., Hirst, W., and Spelke, E. S. (1981). Limited capacity theories and the notion of automaticity: Reply to Lucas and Bub. *Journal of Experimental Psychology: General 110*(4), 499–500.

Norman, D. A. (1969). *Memory and attention: An introduction to human information processing*. New York: John Wiley.

Palazzi, F. (1939). *Nuovissimo dizionario della lingua italiana*. Milano: Ceschina.

Palmonari, A. (1980). Le rappresentazioni sociali. *Giornale Italiano di Psicologia 7*(2), 225–46.

———. (1989). *Processi simbolici e dinamiche sociali*. Bologna: Il Mulino.

———. (Ed.) (1993). *Psicologia dell' adolescenza*. Bologna: Il Mulino.

Pattee, H. H. (1973). *Hierarchy theory. The challenge of complex systems*. New York: Braziller.

Piaget, J. (1954). *The construction of reality in the child.* New York: Basic Books.

———. (1971). *Biology and knowledge.* Chicago: University of Chicago Press.

Polanyi, K. (1944). *The great transformation.* New York: Holt, Rinehart & Winston Inc.

Popper, K. R. (1972). *Objective knowledge. An evolutionary approach.* Oxford: Clarendon Press.

Prigogine, I. (1976). Order through fluctuations. Self-organization and social systems. In E. Jantsch and L. H. Waddington (Eds.), *Evolution and consciousness. Human systems in transition.* Reading, MA: Addison-Wesley.

Rathunde, K. (1988). Family context and optimal experience. In M. Csikszentmihalyi and I. Csikszentmihalyi Selega (Eds.), *Optimal experience. Studies of flow in consciousness.* Cambridge, MA: Cambridge University Press.

———. (1989). The context of optimal experience: An exploratory model of the family. *New Ideas in Psychology* 2(7), 91–97.

———. (1993). The experience of interest: A theoretical and empirical look at its role in adolescent talent development. In P. Pintrich and M. Maehr (Eds.), *Advances in motivation and achievement (Vol. 8). Greenwich, CT: Jai Press.*

Rathunde, K., and Csikszentmihalyi, M. (1991). Adolescent happiness and family interaction. In K. Pillemer and K. McCartney (Eds.), *Parent–child relations throughout life.* Hillsdale: Lawrence Erlbaum.

Reichard, G. A. (1950). *Navajo religion.* Princeton: Princeton University Press, Bollingen Series.

Rigby, C. S., Deci, E. L., Patrick, B. C., and Ryan, R. M. (1992). Beyond the intrinsic–extrinsic dichotomy: Self-determination in motivation and learning. *Motivation and Emotion* 16(3), 165–85.

Rogers, C. (1961). *On becoming a person.* Boston: Houghton, Mifflin.

———. (1963). The actualizing tendency in relation to "motives" and to consciousness. In M. R. Jones (Ed.), *Nebraska symposium on motivation* (Vol. ll). Lincoln: Nebraska University Press.

Rosen, R. (1978) On anticipatory system I: When can a system contain a predictive model? *Journal of Social and Biological Structures* 1(2), 228–44.

Ross, M. (1975). Salience of reward and intrinsic motivation. *Journal of Personality and Social Psychology 32,* 245–54.

Rushdie, S. (1987). *The jaguar smile. A Nicaraguan journey.* New York: Elisabeth Sifton Books, Viking.

149

Ryan, R. M. (1982). Control and information in the intrapersonal sphere: An extension of cognitive evaluation theory. *Journal of Personality and Social Psychology 43*, 450–61.

Ryan, R. M., and Connell, J. P. (1989). Perceived locus of causality and internalization: Examining reasons for acting in two domains. *Journal of Personality and Social Psychology 57*, 749–61.

Ryan, R. M., Connell, J. P., and Deci, E. L. (1985). A motivational analysis of self-determination and self-regulation in education. In C. Ames and R. E. Ames (Eds.), *Research on motivation in education: The classroom milieu*. New York: Academic Press.

Ryan, R. M., Connell, J. P., and Plant, R. W. (1990). Emotions in non-directed text learning. *Learning and Individual Differences 2*, 1–17.

Ryan, R. M., Mims, V., and Koestner, R. (1983). Relation of reward contingency and interpersonal context to intrinsic motivation: A review and test using cognitive evaluation theory. *Journal of Personality and Social Psychology 45*, 736–50.

Ryan, R. M., and Stiller, J. (1991). The social contexts of internalization: Parent and teacher influences on autonomy motivation and learning. In P. R. Pintrich and M. L. Maehr (Eds.), *Advances in motivation and achievement* (Vol. 7), *Goals and self-regulatory processes*. Greenwich: Jai Press.

Sahlins, M. (1976). *The use and abuse of biology. An anthropological critique of sociobiology*. Ann Arbour: University of Michigan Press.

Sato, I. (1988). Bosoku: Flow in Japanese motorcycle gangs. In M. Csikszentmihalyi and I. Csikszentmihalyi Selega (Eds.), *Optimal experience. Studies of flow in consciousness*. Cambridge, MA: Cambridge University Press.

Segall, M. H., Dasen, P. R., Berry, J. W., and Poortinga, Y. H. (1990). *Human behavior in global perspective*. New York: Pergamon Press.

Severi, C. (1992). Le chamanisme et la dame du bon jeu. *L'Homme 121*, 32(1), 165–77.

Shweder, R. A. (1990). Cultural psychology. What is it? In J. W. Stigler, R. A. Shweder, and G. Herdt (Eds.), *Cultural psychology: Essays on comparative human development*. Cambridge, MA: Cambridge University Press.

Shweder, R. A., and Bourne, E. J. (1984). Does the concept of the person vary cross-culturally? In R. A. Shweder and R. A. Levine (Eds.), *Culture theory*. New York: Cambridge University Press.

Simon, H. A. (1988). Creativity and motivation: A response to Csikszentmihalyi. *New Ideas in Psychology 6*(2), 177–81.

Simonton, D. K. (1984a). *Genius, creativity and leadership*. Cambridge: Harvard University Press.

————. (1984b). Artistic creativity and relationships across and within generations. *Journal of Personality and Social Psychology 46*, 1273–1286.

Simpson, J., and Kenrick, D. (Eds.) (1996). *Evolutionary social psychology.* Mahwah, NJ: Lawrence Erlbaum.

Sow, I. (1977). *Psychiatrie dynamique africaine.* Paris: Payot.

Sternberg, R. J. (1988). *The nature of creativity.* New York: Cambridge University Press.

Stigler, J. W., Shweder, R. A., and Herdt, G. (Eds.) (1990). *Cultural psychology: Essays on comparative human development.* Cambridge, MA: Cambridge University Press.

Sue, D. W., Ivery, A. E., and Pedersen, P. B. (1996). *Theory of multicultural counseling and therapy.* Pacific Grove, CA: Brooks/Cole.

Suzuki, L., Meller, P., and Ponterotto, J. (Eds.) (1996). *Handbook of multicultural assessment: Clinical, psychological, and educational applications.* San Francisco, CA: Jossey-Bass.

Tajfel, H. (1981). *Human groups and social categories. Studies in social psychology.* Cambridge: Cambridge University Press.

————. (Ed.) (1982). *Social identity and intergroup relations.* Cambridge, MA: Cambridge University Press.

Tart, C. (1975). *Stati di coscienza.* Roma: Astrolabio.

Taylor, C. (1992). *The ethics of authenticity.* Cambridge: Harvard University Press.

Terranova-Cecchini, R. (1985). Psichiatria transculturale. In *Enciclopedia medica italiana.* Uses Edizioni Scientifiche, Firenze.

————. (1991). L'Io culturale: Luogo del pensiero, luogo dello sviluppo. In P. Inghilleri and R. Terranova-Cecchini (Eds.), *Avanzamenti in psicologia transculturale.* Milano: F. Angeli.

Terranova-Cecchini, R., and Panzeri, L. (1986). *Cooperazione in Nicaragua: La salute mentale. Teoria e pratica di psichiatria transculturale per lo sviluppo.* Milano: Grt.

Treisman, A. M., and Gelade, G. (1980). A feature integration theory of attention. *Cognitive Psychology 12*, 97–136.

Treisman, A. M., and Schmidt, H. (1982). Illusory conjunctions in the perception of objects. *Cognitive Psychology 14*, 107–141.

Triandis, H. C. (1989). The self and social behavior in different cultural contexts. *Psychological Review 96*, 506–520.

————. (1994). *Culture and social behavior.* New York: McGraw-Hill.

Turner, V. (1982). *From the ritual to theatre: The human seriousness of play.* New York: New York Performing Arts Journal Publications.

Ugazio, V. (Ed.) (1988). *La costruzione della conoscenza.* Milano: F. Angeli.

Van Gennep, A. (1909). *Les rites de passage.* Paris: E. Nourry.

151

Volkenstein, M. C., and Chernavskii, D. S. (1978). Information and biology. *Journal of Social and Biological Structures* 1(1), 95–108.

Von Foerster, H. (1985). Cibernetica ed epistemologia. In G. Bocchi and M. Ceruti (Eds.), *La sfida della complessità*. Milano: Feltrinelli.

Watson, R. I. (Ed.) (1979). *Basic writings in the history of psychology*. New York: Oxford University Press.

Weisfeld, G. E. (1993). The adaptive value of humor and laughter. *Ethology and Sociobiology 14,* 141–69.

Wells, A. J. (1986). Variazioni nell'autostima delle madri nei diversi contesti quotidiani: Influenza della presenza dei figli. In F. Massimini and P. Inghilleri (Eds.), *L'esperienza quotidiana. Teoria e metodo di Analisi*. Milano: F. Angeli.

Werner, H. (1948). *Comparative psychology of mental development*. New York: International Universities Press.

Wertsch, J. V., del Rio, P., and Alvarez, A. (Eds.) (1995). *Sociocultural studies of mind*. New York: Cambridge University Press.

White, R. W. (1959). Motivation reconsidered: The concept of competence. *Psychological Review 66,* 297–333.

Wilson, E. O. (1975). *Sociobiology. The new synthesis*. Cambridge, MA: Belknap Press.

Wilson, J. P., and Raphael, B. (Eds.) (1993). *International handbook of traumatic stress syndrome*. New York: Plenum Press.

Yang, K. S., and Bond, M. H. (1990). Exploring implicit personality theories with indigenous or imported constructs: The Chinese case. *Journal of Personality and Social Psychology 56,* 1087–95.

Zuckerman, M. (1979). *Sensation seeking*. Hillsdale: Lawrence Erlbaum.

AUTHOR INDEX

155

SUBJECT INDEX